RFID for the Supply Chain and Operations Professional

RFID for the Supply Chain and Operations Professional

Pamela Zelbst

and

Victor Sower

First published in 2012 by
Business Expert Press, LLC
222 East 46th Street, New York, NY 10017
www.businessexpertpress.com

ISBN-13: 978-1-60649-268-0 (paperback)

ISBN-13: 978-1-60649-269-7 (e-book)

DOI 10.4128/9781606492697

A publication in the Business Expert Press Supply and Operations
Management collection

Collection ISSN: 2156-8189 (print)
Collection ISSN: 2156-8200 (electronic)

Cover design by Jonathan Pennell
Interior design by Scribe Inc.

First edition: February 2012

10 9 8 7 6 5 4 3 2 1

Printed in the United States of America.

Testimonials

This book is the perfect primer for the uninitiated manager struggling to understand RFID technology and how the technology can be used to solve problems related to existing operations and supply chain management. The book is clear and concise and easily understood due to the nontechnical approach adopted by the authors. The reader is introduced to RFID technology and instructed in the essentials and uses of the technology. As the reader begins to appreciate the technology, the authors provide the reader examples of solutions from all sectors. The book is full of excellent examples of how the technology has been used to solve existing problems. The reader will take away an understanding of the capabilities of the technology to improve efficiency, effectiveness, and responsiveness throughout product and service delivery processes. In addition to the plethora of examples, the authors offer several in-depth cases that illustrate successful applications of RFID technology in multiple settings. Once you understand the technology and its potential value, the authors provide a step-by-step approach to successfully implementing RFID systems. Finally, they discuss the future of RFID technology utilization. Essentially, the authors describe how RFID technology can be used to strategic advantage.

Dr. Kenneth Green, Jr.
LeMay Professor of Technology
Southern Arkansas University

This book does a great job of introducing and explaining RFID technology, what makes it work, and the various settings and applications where it can improve process flows. I am now more aware of where I might encounter RFID technology, where and when it could be used to improve processes, and how to add value to an organization.

Mr. Ken Holland
Continuous Improvement Program Manager, Supply Chain Operations
Freescale, Inc.

Abstract

The quality and effectiveness of decisions made within an organization and its supply chain depend on the accuracy and timeliness of the information on which they are based. Radio frequency identification (RFID) is a technology that can provide more accurate information in near real time and thus increase the quality and timeliness of decisions based on that information. RFID systems are currently in use in areas such as inventory management, process control, asset tracking and monitoring, and retail point of sale. Organizations that appropriately incorporate RFID into their operations and information management systems have increased their agility, effectiveness, and efficiency, resulting in organizational growth and increased profitability.

The appropriate utilization of RFID allows organizations to become more agile, resulting in their ability to respond to customers more efficiently and effectively. Technology by itself does not result in improvements, and RFID is no exception. RFID is not a solution for every problem. However, when coupled with other appropriate technologies to address an appropriate objective, RFID can offer a variety of benefits to businesses. The proper integration of RFID into the firm's competitive plans and processes provides the ability to leverage the technology for competitive advantage and results in increased performance for organizations.

The intent of this book is to provide a sufficient discussion of RFID to enable readers with no prior knowledge to develop a basic understanding of the technology. The book discusses current applications and specific examples of RFID usage taken from a variety of industries. The appropriate coupling of RFID with other technologies such as global positioning systems (GPS), enterprise resource planning (ERP), and robotics is discussed as well as an overview of the RFID implementation process. This book will help readers develop an understanding of the capability of the technology to increase an organization's customer responsiveness.

Keywords

RFID; effectiveness; efficiency; timeliness; agility; inventory management; asset tracking; real-time information systems; RFID integration; RFID implementation; customer responsiveness.

Contents

Illustrations

Tables

Figures

Box

Abbreviations and Acronyms

ADC	automatic data capture
AFSP	average factory selling price
AIDC	automatic identification and data capture
AII	auto ID infrastructure
AIM	Association for Automatic Identification and Mobility
AIT	automatic information technology
ANSI	American National Standards Institute
aRFID	active radio frequency identification
CNC	computer numerical control
DARPA	Defense Advanced Research Projects Agency
DLA	Defense Logistics Agency
DOD	Department of Defense
EAS	electronic article surveillance
EM	event management
EMEA	Europe, the Middle East, and Africa
EMV	Europay MasterCard Visa
EPC	Electronic Product Code
ERP	enterprise resource planning
ETSI	European Telecommunications Standards Institute
FCC	Federal Communications Commission
FLC	foldable large container
GPS	global positioning system
HF	high frequency
ISO	International Organization for Standardization
ITV	in-transit visibility
KPI	key performance indicators
LCD	liquid crystal display
LF	low frequency
LIMS	laboratory information management system
LPs	long plays
MHz	megahertz
NIST	National Institute of Standards and Technology
OR	operating room

PIN	personal identification number
POS	point-of-sale
pRFID	passive radio frequency identification
RFID	radio frequency identification
ROI	return on investment
SCM	supply chain management
SDK	software development kit
UHF	ultra high frequency
USTRANSCOM	U.S. Transportation Command
VMI	vendor managed inventory
WIP	work-in-progress inventory
WMS	warehouse management system

Acknowledgments

The authors would like to acknowledge the peer reviewers of the manuscript for this book for their careful review and helpful comments:

- Dr. Kenneth Green, LeMay professor of technology, Southern Arkansas University
- Mr. Ken Holland, continuous improvement program manager, supply chain operations, Freescale, Inc.
- Mr. George Dyche, product manager, Avery Dennison Corp.

We would like to thank Mr. Scott Isenberg, principal and consultant at CounselPub Publishing Services, who provided us the opportunity to undertake the writing of this book, and the editorial staff at Business Expert Press, who worked with us to turn our manuscript into a finished product.

Lastly, we would like to acknowledge and thank our spouses, Charles and Judy, for their support and encouragement during the process of writing this book.

CHAPTER 1

RFID Basics

On a recent international trip, one of the authors parked in a long-term parking facility near the airport that provides an identification card to frequent parkers. When I arrived at the parking facility, I placed my card against a reader. My name immediately appeared on an LCD display and the attendant addressed me by name when she directed me to my parking space. When returning, again I placed my card against a reader, which displayed my name, the number of days I had been parked, and the amount due. I paid my bill by swiping my credit card without speaking to an attendant. Any frequent parker specials were automatically credited to my bill. This was made possible by a radio frequency identification (RFID) tag embedded in the frequent parkers' identification card. The only information recorded on the tag was a coded number, which matched my name in a protected database.

When I went through the customs and border security stations in the international airport, I was required to present my passport. The security agent saw my picture on a monitor along with other identifying information to ensure that I am who I say I am, that I am using a valid passport, and that I am not on any watch lists. This was made possible by the RFID tag embedded in my passport.

On the drive home from the airport I used the toll road. An E-ZPass transponder made it a breeze to speed through special lanes at the toll booths. The toll authority registered my passage and automatically billed my account. This too is made possible by an RFID tag, which is embedded in the E-ZPass transponder.

Returning home I was greeted by Buddy, my dog. He has an RFID chip implanted in his neck that is encoded with a number that is tied to me in a database to identify him should he wander away from home.

The point is, believe it or not, *you are already using RFID in your personal life.* And each of these uses shows that businesses and governmental agencies are also using RFID technology in order to increase efficiency, gain a competitive advantage, increase security, or provide a service that is better than could be otherwise provided.

Perhaps your organization has not explored the possibilities that RFID technology has for improving performance and reducing cost. Perhaps your competitors have.

Civilian businesses and the military are already using RFID. The U.S. Army uses active RFID tags and a variety of sensors to monitor temperature, shock, unauthorized entry, and various other critical data for shipments to war zones. A tortilla manufacturer saved $700,000 in packaging costs by tracking shipping containers using RFID.[1] Marathon Oil Company estimated that using RFID on their downhole drilling tools would result in a savings of $17 million and improve operational safety for their employees.[2] Libraries are locating misshelved books simply by walking through the stacks with a portable RFID reader. Many organizations are using RFID to simplify asset management. With RFID it is possible to inventory all tagged assets in a room in a matter of minutes

Figure 1.1. The value of RFID.

Photograph courtesy of the Sower Business Technology Laboratory, College of Business Administration, Sam Houston State University

without searching for a printed asset tag or bar code label seemingly affixed to the most inaccessible spot on the asset.

The apparel industry is adopting this technology at an extremely fast pace because RFID creates a real-time information environment allowing for decision making using current information. Using RFID, apparel inventories can be monitored in the back room to track when an item arrives and when it moves to the retailer's floor. The real-time information system can be extended to the sales floor to track inventory as it is purchased so that information is updated automatically, keeping records current in real time. Savvy retailers can use the information to identify which items are moving quickly and keep the floor stocked so that sales can increase. The technology can provide an advantage in vendor managed inventory (VMI) systems. Automated inventory management allows vendors to have real-time information resulting in fewer stockouts. In addition the retailers' cost for holding safety stock is reduced.

Health care organizations are also widely using RFID technologies. Hospitals are using RFID, for example, to track specialized equipment, such as medication pumps, incubators, and wheelchairs, to assure that surgical implements are all accounted for prior to suturing a surgical patient in the operating room, to assist in the prevention of medication errors, and to ensure that newborns are not removed from the nursery without authorization. Nursing homes are monitoring the location of Alzheimer's patients with RFID.

RFID can be used as a stand-alone system or as a part of integrated systems that may, for example, include bar codes, global positioning software, environmental sensors, and many other parts. RFID has the potential to add value by providing increased visibility to supply chains; however, suppliers who are mandated to tag items for a retail customer often find it difficult to see the value that RFID can bring internally. Manufacturers are adopting the technology to track assets, materials, and employees. When utilizing RFID for at least a 6-month period, manufacturers identified an average cycle-time reduction of 19%, a reduction in safety stock requirements of 27%, and an improvement in changeover time of 24%. RFID can be integrated into just about any industry and supply chain.[3] The greatest value that the technology has to offer is the flexibility to make decisions in real time.

Structure of the Book

This book provides readers who have little or no knowledge of RFID technology the basic background needed to begin considering how this technology can contribute to the success of their organizations. It also provides examples of how other organizations are using the technology.

In chapter 2 we provide the basic technical details about RFID and how it works. A basic knowledge of the technical aspects of RFID is essential in order to understand its capabilities and how they might be part of the solution to problems you are trying to address. This knowledge also is essential for being able to communicate better with manufacturers, suppliers, systems integrators, consultants, and others who might be essential to enabling your organization to take advantage of the technology.

Later in the book, we bring you up to date on the state of the technology, its current applications, and future possibilities. Of course there are few boundaries on the uses of RFID, so if you do not see a discussion of the application you have in mind, then yours might be the next innovative use of the technology, which means you could create an advantage over others in your industry who have not yet conceived of that application.

We include in the book a selection of four business cases that provide some detail about actual organizations that have developed applications for RFID. The cases provide insight into how a diverse group of organizations went from idea to implemented process and the effect the new process had on organizational performance. We then discuss the process of implementation and what is next for RFID in the coming years.

Hanns-Christian L. Hanebeck's essay (immediately following this section) addresses the value of RFID. Over the past two decades, Chris has focused his career on management consulting, strategy development, and technology innovation. He currently serves as vice president of product management and marketing at Revere Security, where his responsibilities include the design and implementation of innovative data, and privacy protection solutions for small, resource-constrained wireless devices that range from smart meters to RFID tags.

Prior to his work at Revere, Chris ran his own management consulting firm, led the industrial sector consulting group for RFID at IBM, and spent 6 years in several executive roles at GlobeRanger, an innovative software startup for RFID Edgeware. Chris has successfully completed business process redesign and software implementation projects for more than 60 clients on three continents exceeding $65 million in overall budget responsibility.

Chris has authored over 50 publications, presented at over 75 major conferences, and has been awarded two U.S. patents with an additional seven IBM patent applications pending. He holds an MBA from the University of Saarbrucken in Germany and teaches supply chain strategy at the University of North Texas. He can be reached at hhanebeck@yahoo.com.

The Value of RFID

by Hanns-Christian L. Hanebeck,
VP of Product Management and Marketing,
Revere Security

The auto-ID industry has matured considerably over the past few years. We have seen many innovative applications, specifically for RFID, in fields that we did not even begin to imagine in the late 1990s when UHF technology first took off. Still, we need to ask ourselves periodically where the underlying value of RFID technology for users really lies. On the surface, RFID is an identification technology that allows the collection of large amounts of data in a fast and efficient way. Obviously tags can be placed on items, cartons, pallets, or even shipping containers, which can be read as soon as they pass an RFID gate, scanned with a handheld, or transported on a forklift with RFID antennae. Unfortunately most of the resulting data an RFID system captures is either redundant or obvious. If a company plans to ship 10 pallets of its product to a customer and actually does so, then the RFID system has little value beyond knowing that warehouse personnel have just properly followed procedures. While this knowledge can be valuable in itself, the advantage of RFID to monitor business processes will not be utilized very much. However, as soon as exceptions occur, the value proposition for RFID changes drastically. Now the technology can become a deterrent of errors where other technologies, such as barcodes, fail since they require that each item, carton, or pallet is physically touched. The ability to prevent mistakes and errors before they occur obviously stems from the automated nature of RFID. There was a good example a few years ago when a large U.S. automaker began to track tradeshow displays through RFID after they had mixed up two trucks—one going to their largest annual auto show and the other going to a small-town exhibition. The effects of this simple mistake were far-reaching and obviously the cost to remedy it was much higher than the cost for the implementation of an RFID system to prevent misshipments before they happen. In addition, we have seen substantial labor savings in virtually all industries through the automation of business processes and the elimination of clipboards and barcode scanners.

This case serves as a good example of how RFID technology can generate business value by deterring mistakes. Mistakes happen in daily processes, just as things are lost or stolen. We cannot always change the human element and it is difficult, as well as costly, to design and implement sufficient business controls to reduce errors to an acceptable level in many cases. This is where RFID plays a crucial role; it allows users to identify exceptions and manage business processes much more efficiently. This simple ability leads to a fundamental shift in how processes are managed: we move away from managing all aspects of a process, such as supervising an entire operation, to mainly managing exceptions. In other words, for process applications we should expect RFID to provide the ability to manage errors and processes that could break down.

A second aspect of RFID is equally valuable: its ability to scan things quickly and from a distance without line of sight, which allows us to locate items efficiently. Libraries and book stores are great examples of applications that can take advantage of this aspect of RFID. As soon as a book is misplaced, perhaps because someone took it out of one shelf location and displaced it onto another, it becomes the ominous needle in the haystack. It is virtually impossible to find a misplaced book unless someone performs a manual check by looking at every book on every shelf. Through the use of RFID tags, this process can be handled quickly and efficiently by a clerk using a handheld device to scan through rows of books to identify misplaced items. The system on the handheld reader only needs to know which shelf it is scanning and what should be expected in terms of tag reads on that shelf. The same is true for other, related fields such as government offices, law firms, hospitals, and medical practices—all of which need to manage large amounts of documents and files that are subject to being misplaced.

Finding the needle in the haystack does not necessarily have to be just a remedy to mistakes. In many yard applications for example, RFID provides an efficient way to locate items that range from cars to ocean containers. There is a very substantial business case behind this capability. The Defense Advanced Research Projects Agency (DARPA) has estimated that the cost of not being able to efficiently locate shipping containers that were dropped into "desert warehouses" during the first Gulf War cost the U.S. military roughly $740 million throughout the war. This figure includes the cost of double orders placed by commanders in the field who would reorder supplies to be shipped to the troops directly, when they did not receive the first order in time. Here, the effects of a lack of trust become apparent in that doubts about the reliability of a supply chain quickly lead to excess inventory and thus unnecessary cost.

Both the avoidance of errors and the ability to locate something have a common basis often referred to as "visibility." RFID enables us to obtain granular data, convert it into meaningful information, and share the resulting knowledge with the right people in the organization so that they can ultimately make the right decisions. When we design applications, it is thus important to focus on those issues that are most pressing, can save the most money, or have the greatest impact on a company. This point was poignantly made at a Zeitgeist event, the Google user conference, where Google cofounder Larry Page stated that his company will only focus on what he called "toothbrush problems." He defined a toothbrush as an item that people spend more time with than most other items during a given day. Obviously what he meant was that his company, while not literally reinventing the toothbrush, should focus on those applications that impact people the most, such as consuming vital information, using mobile phones, or operating a vehicle. For RFID solution designers and implementers, the toothbrush problem is one that can be solved efficiently, has lasting, sustainable effects, and touches a business in substantial ways.

What is important is that we often have the luxury to measure the impact of RFID technology on a company or organization through its return on investment (ROI). Hence the best business cases can quickly become the biggest toothbrush. Of course, we have to keep in mind that innovative applications, and those that touch consumers, may not be as easily quantifiable. These are often the toothbrushes we did not know existed before a solution has been implemented.

In the automotive industry, for example, there are several dozen meaningful applications for RFID technology across business processes. The key is not so much to define each and every one in detail, but to see past this variety of possible applications to focus on a few pressing issues and high-return applications such as returnable container management, yard management, and manufacturing automation opportunities. While there are substantial opportunities in customer-facing processes at the dealership, these may not be the first opportunities to pursue due to the justified lure of more attractive financial gains in manufacturing automation. On the other hand, in the hotel and resort industry there are well over 20 meaningful applications for RFID, and the ones that stand out are all related to customer ease of use such as access to rooms and facilities, automation of the check-in and check-out process, as well as automation of payments. While these may not have a strictly quantifiable business case, the same was true when American Airlines invented Sabre, the first real-time airline reservation system, almost 40 years ago. It was initially built on the belief that the airline could reinvent a business process, that of booking travel, in a way that gave it a distinct competitive advantage. Obviously, we know today that they have succeeded far beyond all expectations and created significant value for the organization.

Another case in point is the approach an innovative retailer in the fashion and apparel industry might take. Specifically it is the novel use of touch screen displays and computing technology within sleek RFID in-store portals to create unique customer experiences. A young, affluent customer walks up to the portal where her store loyalty card is read. The screen now changes from displaying a sequence of advertisements to a web page where the customer can interact with the store system, for example, by accessing her "wish list," see what her friends (if they permit access) have recently bought, access the store inventory in her size, and obtain more detailed information about specific products. She will also be able to send messages to and receive them from her friends, view the comments that other people have made about products that she is interested in, and many other applications that no one has imagined yet. Last, but not least, she can retrieve recommendations about related products, such as sunglasses or belts, that match what she intends to buy or has already purchased. It is not inconceivable that the store might offer discounts based on the frequency with which she posts her own comments and responds to those of others. It goes without saying that the customer should be able to pay with her loyalty card as long as it is connected to a credit card and personal identification number (PIN) and also that, one day, she should be able to place her loyalty card on an inexpensive RFID reader connected to her home PC to access the features outside of the physical store locations. This is just one of many examples for the transformational promise of RFID when process efficiency is coupled with innovation to enhance the consumer experience.

Returning to process efficiency benefits, we should not overlook an important quality in RFID technology that is often less noticed or even neglected in initial implementations. Namely it has the ability to enable insight into complex business processes through low-cost sampling. In fact, RFID has provided this type of capability since the mid-1990s in a number of industries. The technology provides a strong mechanism to enhance process visibility and measurements of performance outside of the immediate effects that the technology itself has on an operation. In this role, RFID technology can help facilitate meaningful process changes to reduce inefficiency and error by providing data that were previously unavailable. The technology allows users to assess and document operational performance on a very granular level thus creating value beyond the initial technology implementation.

An excellent example is the active RFID implementation at International Post Corporation, which began in 1994. Their system has been deployed in more than 50 countries, boasts over 10,000 read points and uses roughly 600,000 active RFID tags today. What is interesting about the system is not just its early date but, more importantly, that the postal industry understood the fundamental value proposition of RFID to streamline business processes and identify challenges in the flow of goods and materials. In this particular implementation, test letters containing RFID tags are sent along with regular mail in very much the same way that inspection pigs are used to inspect pipelines: tagged letters float among the broad stream of normal ones to ensure that the whole system works well. The resulting data allows all participating postal carriers to identify where business processes break down and to draw meaningful conclusions about why specific problems have evolved. This use of RFID technology provides the information needed by postal carriers to improve their operations by assessing the performance of the global supply chain for correspondence through accurate, reliable, and unbiased performance measures. One of the inherent advantages is that it provides factual data to decision makers who no longer have to rely on guesswork and intuition. The technology thus takes subjectivity out of the argument allowing participants in the system to assess and remedy inefficiencies without emotion. This ability to contribute to performance measurements has long been an interesting value proposition that experienced implementers and users look for when they deploy RFID systems. When viewed in the light of this RFID capability, even compliance mandates can potentially become very attractive for suppliers as long as data are shared along the entire supply chain.

> **Side Note 1.1**
>
> Infosphere™ Traceability Server is an information sharing platform for traceability. This server allows for traceability applications that create real-time visibility events. These servers can be used with RFID for business and supply chain processes. (IBM Traceability Server Overview)

To realize the benefits of performance assessments in RFID systems, the resulting data need to be used in dashboards and business intelligence applications. One example of a mature dashboard for RFID applications is the Infosphere™ Traceability Server offered by IBM. The Infosphere™ Traceability Server systems allow for the continuous monitoring of operational performance, and IBM provides a platform to analyze the data for reporting purposes on an as-needed basis. Every information technology implementation, not just RFID, is only as good as the resulting data and the ability to act on the information derived from that data. In order to accomplish this, it is important to generate the data consistently, reliably, and in an automated fashion. Every gap and uncertainty in the data lead to second-guessing and will eventually destroy the necessary trust. This implies that RFID systems need to be designed in a way that substantially reduces or eliminates false positive reads. It also means that data have to be delivered consistently. The system needs to be set up so that it continually feeds into user-defined key performance indicators (KPI), which provide meaningful insights to process designers and decision makers. The KPIs can be built along multiple dimensions and, ideally, the data are fed into the business intelligence system in near real time. In this manner, suboptimal performance expressed by throughput times, rest times, or missed opportunities (for example too early or too late shipments) becomes apparent. On a broader level, additional performance measures about cost, quality, and flexibility can be collected or inferred. The resulting information is invaluable when it comes to business process redesign and optimization activities. The changes facilitated by the information provided by the system can yield cost and time reductions, as well as increases in quality and flexibility, and generate tangible savings to provide an additional level of value that would have been hard, if not impossible, to attain without the use of RFID technology.

In summary, it is important to identify the effects that visibility has on a process before RFID is used to solve a problem. Visibility leads to confidence, which in turn leads to tangible savings. Any application designer should identify these savings before the technology is implemented. The key, obviously, is to maintain a focus on applications that create a strong ROI or have a high impact on customer-facing activities. At the same time, investments in RFID infrastructure often allow for secondary and tertiary application opportunities, which leverage the same infrastructure and thus have a far lower financial hurdle in order to achieve a lasting and solid

ROI. There are probably dozens of such issues in the industry, which we have yet to uncover. The task for RFID application designers and implementers is to identify and implement them swiftly. The motto for RFID technology thus becomes to "think big, start small, and move fast."

CHAPTER 2

RFID Technology Essentials

RFID was a $5 million global industry in 2009 and is forecast to become a $4 billion industry by 2019.[1] For this forecast to materialize, the cost of the RFID tags will need to come down to a price of less than 1 cent. While at today's prices RFID provides a positive return on investment (ROI) for high-cost items, the key to justification for using the technology for low-cost items is a lower tag price. However, given this forecast, and the progress being made to reduce tag prices, the need to begin thinking about how RFID fits into your organization becomes apparent. Before you can take the first step in determining how the technology fits with your organizational needs, you must first develop a general understanding of how the technology works.

RFID works by transmitting information encoded on an RFID tag via radio waves to a reader and then to a computer database from which information can be utilized in the making of timely and even automated decisions. An RFID system typically comprises a computer, a database, RFID software, RFID readers, RFID antennas, and RFID tags (transponders) and is frequently integrated with other systems within the organization (Figure 2.1). The RFID tag has an antenna for signal receipt and transmission and a microchip for data storage and managing the receipt and transmission of data (Figure 2.2). The RFID reader communicates with a population of tags and sequentially reads the information from the tags very rapidly.

The system is controlled by software installed on a computer. In the case of a passive RFID tag system, a signal is sent out through the system to the antenna via a radio wave. The radio wave reaches the antenna on the RFID tag, which subsequently powers up the microchip on the tag (Figure 2.1). The unique identifier on the microchip is then transmitted back from the tag to the reader's antenna. The middleware on the computer then allows this information to be stored in a database. An active

RFID tag system works in the same way except that it contains its own power source rather than relying on the radio frequency signal from the reader for power.

Until recently, all RFID systems needed middleware to act as a conduit to get the information into the database. A current trend is toward intelligent RFID readers that eliminate the need for middleware so that the information can be transmitted directly into a database. Most RFID systems now come with a development package that allows the operator to develop a custom program to import the data into a database. Most of these packages are relatively easy to use but some users may want to hire a programmer, which will add to the cost of implementation. In some cases, depending on the brand of reader, middleware software may still be necessary to transmit the information received from the reader to a database.

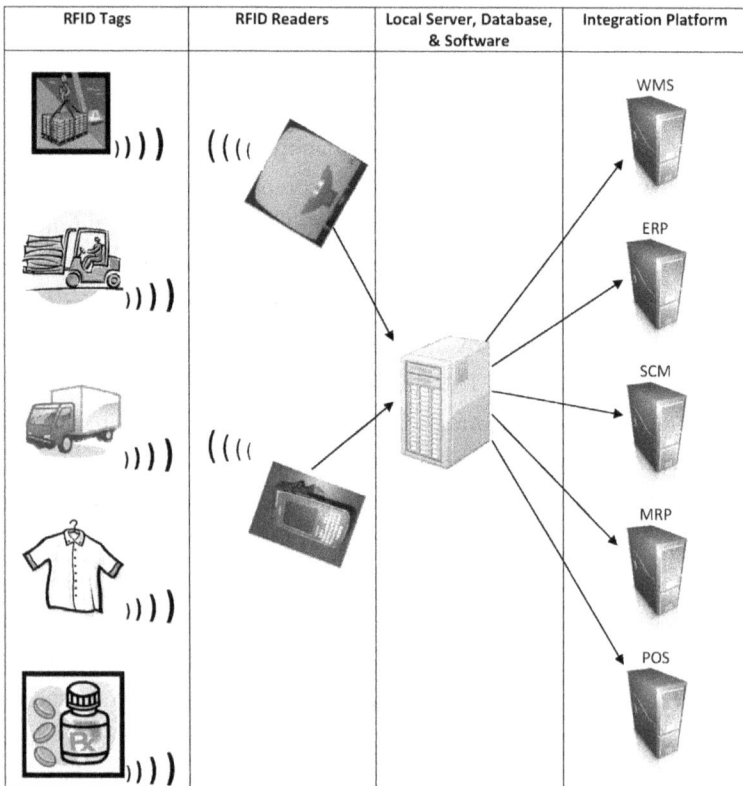

Figure 2.1. How an RFID system works.

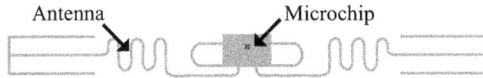

Figure 2.2. Anatomy of an RFID tag.

Photograph courtesy of Venture Research, Inc. Used with permission.

Another trend is toward cloud computing. A company can use cloud computing as an alternative to setting up and maintaining their own server and software on site. Cloud computing allows a user to access their information from a server that is hosted in a different location (Figure 2.3). This eliminates the need to invest in expensive infrastructure, such as a server. There are three forms of cloud computing offered as services through a remote provider: infrastructure, platform, and software.[2] An example of an infrastructure service is storage to backup a home or business computer. A platform service example is providing the ability for users to create their own applications. Software services provided through cloud computing include running software applications through the Internet rather than purchasing the application for individual computers.

The most important parameters of an RFID system and the technology requirements revolve around the distance between the reader and the tag, the amount of time to complete a transaction, and reader access to a network to store related data. To understand the importance of these parameters, a basic understanding of the elements of a system and how it works is necessary. The following information will provide that basic understanding.

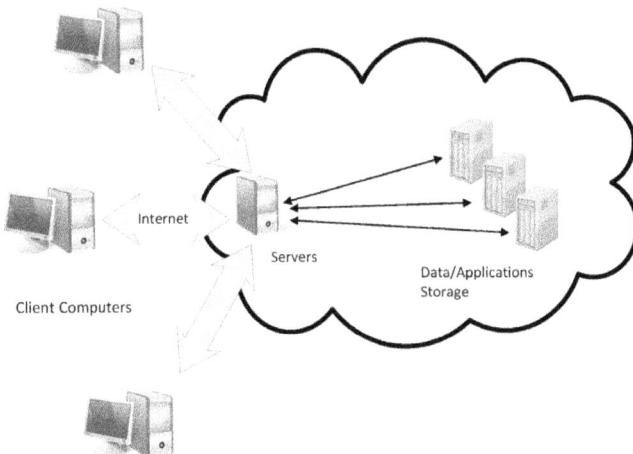

Figure 2.3. Cloud computing.

Types of RFID

The U.S. Department of Defense can track the movement of military and civilian personnel throughout buildings using RFID tags contained within identification cards and an array of readers throughout the buildings. Some credit card companies utilize RFID technology that allows users to wave their credit cards in front of a reader without having to swipe the cards. Other systems allow the entire contents of tractor-trailer containers to be read as they pass under an RFID antenna on the highway without requiring the vehicle to stop or even slow down. While these are all examples of RFID technologies, they represent different types of that technology. There are two major types of RFID technology, active and passive.

The difference between an active and a passive RFID system is twofold. The first is that an active tag has a power source that is capable of always transmitting a signal, whereas a passive tag has to receive the radio wave in order to power the chip. The second difference is that an active tag can store more information than a passive tag. An active tag has a much shorter life than a passive tag because the power source will eventually deplete itself. The more information stored on the active tag the shorter the lifespan of the tag. However, the signal emitted can be remotely turned off or on and the rate of transmission of the signal can be adjusted to extend the life of an active tag. Additionally some active tags are also intelligent tags that have integrated sensors for such things as temperature and humidity. These sensors may have the capability of monitoring and taking action according to parameters that are programmed into the tag.

Passive systems include low frequency (LF), high frequency (HF), and ultra high frequency (UHF). LF and HF are commonly used for security purposes, while UHF is used primarily for inventory management (Table 2.1). The tags used for passive systems do not have a power supply and cannot send out a signal until the radio wave is received through the antenna supplying power to the microchip on the tag.

A current trend is to use a combination of RFID systems to ensure tracking and matching ability. For example, some companies in the pharmaceutical industry are using HF to tag items such as containers of medicine and LF for employees so that they can match the identification

Table 2.1. Passive RFID Uses

Tag type	Uses*
Low frequency (LF) 125 KHz	Livestock, event tickets, hotel room keys, pet tracking
High frequency (HF) 13.56 MHz	Identification cards, pharmaceuticals
Ultra high frequency (UHF) 860–960 MHz	Inventory control, distribution centers, product authentication

*Each type of passive RFID can be used in most industries in multiple ways. These are examples of how some organizations are using passive RFID systems.

of the employee that possesses a container of medication, adding another level of security. RFID can also be used to combat knockoffs of products. For example, a company producing electric toothbrushes offshore hired a research company to find a way to use RFID internally in their product. This RFID application allowed the company to identify a member of their supply chain who was producing a knockoff of their product and stealing some of their market share (J. Baker, Venture Research, Inc., interview with author, November 9, 2010).

RFID Readers

There are many types of RFID readers, but not all readers are created equal. Some operate better in a dense environment where there are multiple tags stacked on top of one another, while others are more user friendly. A key issue for RFID is the environment in which the reader operates. Harsher environments demand a more durable reader. For example, Plano, Texas–based Venture Research, Inc. makes specific readers for a file-folder tracking system and for a fork lift. Internally there is very little difference between the two. Externally the casing is different to allow for more protection in the more rugged forklift environment (J. Baker, Venture Research, Inc., interview with author, November 9, 2010). Most readers offer the capability of adjusting the power of the radio wave coming out of the antenna for longer or shorter read ranges and the timing of the reads as well. This capability can be useful to control the read zone to prevent reading tags outside the intended zone.

UHF passive readers operate at different frequencies depending on the region of the world that the organization utilizing the technology is located (Table 2.2). The RFID world is divided into three regions with governing bodies that determine the frequencies in each of these areas. However, consistency between these three regions and the regulations governing RFID is currently lacking. An RFID system for one region does not necessarily work in the other two regions. For example, Region 2 (the Americas) uses a frequency span of 902–928 MHz, while Region 1 (Europe) uses a frequency span of 865–867 MHz, making the equipment used in the two regions incompatible. Further, Region 3 (Asia Pacific) does not have a standard frequency span. Japan uses 952–954 MHz, while Singapore uses a frequency span of 920–925MHz (Figure 2.4).

The difference in frequency spans makes it very difficult for RFID to work in a global environment, which limits its capabilities in global supply chains. To combat this issue, research by companies such as Parallax is focused on creating a world tag (Figure 2.5a) that can be read by all UHF passive systems in any region at any frequency (Table 2.2). Avery Dennison and Impinj are also able to provide inlays and tags that can be read in a global environment (860–960 MHz; Figure 2.5b).

Table 2.2. Frequencies Across the World

Regions	Frequencies
1 (Europe and Africa)	865.6–867.6 MHz
2 (North and South America)	902–928 MHz
3 (Asia Pacific)	No specifications

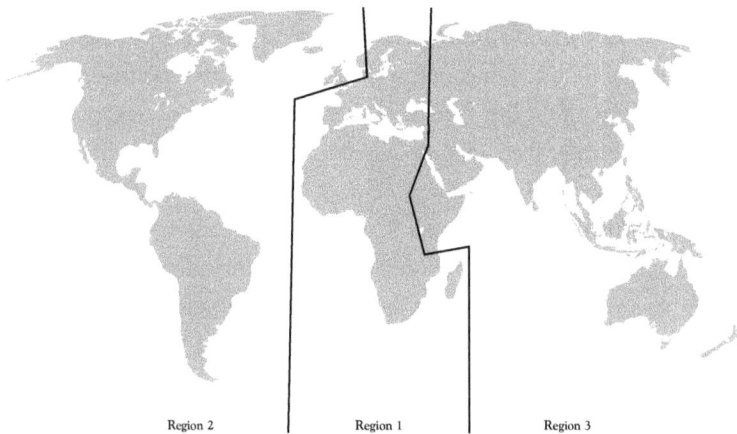

| Region 2 | Region 1 | Region 3 |

Figure 2.4. Three regions of the world.

Figure 2.5a. Parallax world tag.

Photograph courtesy of the Sower Business Technology Laboratory, College of Business Administration, Sam Houston State University.

Figure 2.5b. Avery Dennison AD-827 (performs across the 860–960 MHz frequency).

Photograph courtesy of the Sower Business Technology Laboratory, College of Business Administration, Sam Houston State University.

Tags

There are several classes of RFID tags (Table 2.3). The class of tags indicates the capacity of the tag for certain functions, such as write or rewrite capability. In addition the class can also indicate whether the tag is active and can emit a signal on its own (it has a power supply) or is passive and cannot (antenna and chip only). The most commonly used UHF passive tag is a Class 1 Gen 2. These tags come in many different sizes at varying costs from a large number of suppliers. Selection of the tag will depend on the intended use and the operating environment. There are several considerations when deciding which tag is the right tag for the job:

- The type of passive system in use (LF, HF, or UHF)
- The cost of the tag
- The level of tagging (item, case, pallet)
- The placement of the tag
- The length of the antenna on the tag
- The unique identifier

There are a variety of tags and formats available. For example, some tags come preprogrammed with a number, while others have nothing encoded and the organization must encode the tag before use. The latter types of tags can generally be programmed by holding the tag over the reader while the desired identifier is entered into the reader and then encoded on the tag (Figure 2.6). Organizations wanting to use both bar codes and RFID have the option of using an RFID printer encoder to simultaneously produce the bar code and encode the RFID tag with the same number.

Table 2.3. Classes of Tags

Classes of tags	
Class 0	Read only
Class 1	Write once, read many
Class 2	Rewritable
Class 3	Semipassive
Class 4	Active
Class 5	Reader

Figure 2.6. Zebra RZ400 printer encoder which simultaneously prints RFID, bar code, and text labels.

Photograph courtesy of the Sower Business Technology Laboratory, College of Business Administration, Sam Houston State University.

Types of Passive Tags

The RFID user must first identify the type of system best suited for the organizational needs. Passive tags can be separated into three types based on frequencies. For example, if the user wants to provide secure access to a facility, an LF system might be best. With an LF system, the person wanting to gain entry into a facility would need a card with an LF tag, which must be held within an inch of the reader's antenna in order for it to be read (Figure 2.7). LF tags are more secure from unauthorized reading and cloning since the read distance is limited, which is a desirable characteristic for keycard RFID systems.

HF tags are used in the pharmaceutical industry to lessen the chance of mistakes in dispensing drugs. HF tags must be within 6 in. of the reader's antenna to be read (Figure 2.8). The most commonly used passive tag is an ultrahigh frequency system (UHF), with a Gen 2 Class 1 tag being the most popular (Figure 2.9). These tags can be read from more than 40 ft. away depending on the attenuation of the reader and the length of the antenna on the tag as well as the obstacles that may be encountered. Some of the common obstacles that may be encountered can include metal, cardboard, liquids, and other RFID systems or technologies that are on the same frequencies. For example, metal will reflect or bounce the signal, creating an obstacle in reading the information on the tag. Some liquids can absorb the signal, preventing it from passing through, resulting in the inability to read the information on a tag. Cardboard absorbs humidity and can create an

Figure 2.7. Low frequency RFID system. Clockwise from left: Computer with middleware and database, LF RFID reader, three types of LF RFID tags.

Photograph courtesy of the Sower Business Technology Laboratory, College of Business Administration, Sam Houston State University.

Figure 2.8. High frequency RFID system. Clockwise from left: Computer with middleware and database, HF RFID reader, two types of HF RFID tags.

Photograph courtesy of the Sower Business Technology Laboratory, College of Business Administration, Sam Houston State University.

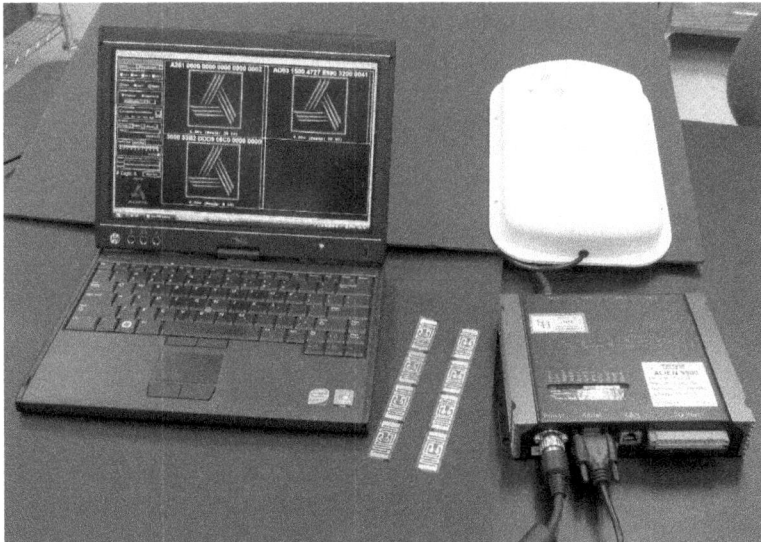

Figure 2.9. Ultrahigh frequency RFID system. Clockwise from left: Computer with middleware and database, UHF RFID antenna, UHF RFID reader, two strips of 4 HF RFID tags.

Photograph courtesy of the Sower Business Technology Laboratory, College of Business Administration, Sam Houston State University.

obstacle because of the liquid absorbed, resulting in the same effect as water. Other RFID systems could leak RFID power and deteriorate a signal; this effect is called a spurious emission. Another issue could be other technologies, such as wireless phone systems, that use the same frequency span and can create an obstacle to obtaining information from an RFID tag.

Gen 2 Class 1 tags are used in a multitude of ways in inventory control to help identify how many of each item is in inventory, if the items are secure, and how many are sold to monitor the availability of items for purchase.

Cost of Tags

The price of tags has been coming down over the past few years, as shown in Figure 2.10. LF and HF tags tend to be more expensive than UHF tags. As previously stated, UHF passive RFID systems are the most commonly used, in part, because UHF passive tags are priced more economically than other types of tags; however they are still too expensive for most item-level tagging applications.

Research in RFID tags has focused primarily on UHF passive technology in recent years. Rice University and a Korean company are experimenting with ink-jet printer technology and nanotubes to produce

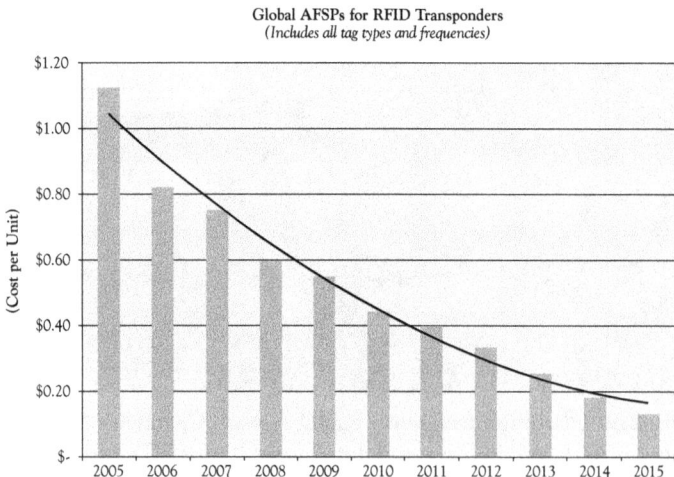

Figure 2.10. Global average factory selling prices for RFID tags.

AFSP is average factory selling price and includes all frequencies. Data from 2005–2011 is actual; 2012–2015 is forecasted. Graph courtesy of VDC Research Group. Used with permission.

a tag that is 3 sq. cm in size and is low in cost.[3] The research has yielded a tag that costs 4 cents, but the ultimate goal of the research is to produce a tag that costs less than 1 cent.[4]

Level of Tagging

Tagging may be done at the pallet, case, and item levels, but most tagging occurs at the pallet and case level because tagging at the item level is still cost prohibitive except for high-value items. Some companies use a license-plate approach where they use RFID tags at the case level and bar codes at the pallet level. The apparel industry is tagging more frequently at the item level but usually for items that are valued over $5.00.

Another reason for utilizing multiple levels would be security. For example, in the pharmaceutical industry, highly controlled medications as well as the personnel handling the product may be tagged. This method allows for association of the medication with the personnel handling it, giving management better control over their products.

Tag Placement

Tag placement is important, especially when items are densely stored or stacked. Items that have tags in the same location can cause an issue called shadowing. Shadowing occurs when a passive tag is not activated because other tags stacked on top are shadowing tags and the antenna from the reader is not able to power up all the tags. However, both Avery Dennison and Impinj market a UHF passive tag specifically designed for dense environments to minimize the chances of this happening (Figure 2.11).

Figure 2.11. Avery Dennison AD-230 UHF tag.

Photograph courtesy of the Sower Business Technology Laboratory, College of Business Administration, Sam Houston State University.

Tag Antenna

RFID tags have two components, a microchip and an antenna. The antenna on the tag can be coiled on the tag to give a longer read range. A heuristic is that the length of the antenna on the tag needs to be at least one-fourth of the distance from the antenna for the readers to read the tags consistently. For example, if the distance from the tag to the reader is 4 ft., then the antenna on the tag would need to be 1 ft. long when stretched out. Otherwise, the signal would not reach the microchip to give it power to transmit the information needed. Recent advances in chip technology enable tag manufacturers to produce smaller tags with increased read ranges. Read ranges are also dependent on the material makeup of the item tagged and its environment.

Unique Identifier

An Electronic Product Code (EPC) associates a tag with a unique serial number, allowing a specific item, place of origin, date of production, and other information to be revealed by utilizing RFID technology to populate a database. A microchip on a basic passive tag can hold 96 bits of information (Figure 2.12). Once these 96 bits of information are communicated back to the reader, the information can be stored in a database, and the unique identifier can be associated with other information in the database, such as name of the item, place of origin, and so forth. Each microchip has four banks of information: Bank 0, Bank 1, Bank 2, and Bank 3 (Table 2.4).[5]

Although 96 bits of information are very common today, many chip manufacturers have developed tags with EPC memories of 128 bits, 240 bits, and 496 bits. Some UHF chips provide memory as high as 512 bits and 640 bits in addition to the EPC memory for the storage of such additional information as date, time, and product identification.

Reader Antennas

Reader antennas come in all shapes and sizes. Much like readers, antennas can be in different casings depending on the requirements of the environment. Some readers have an internal antenna, while other readers use

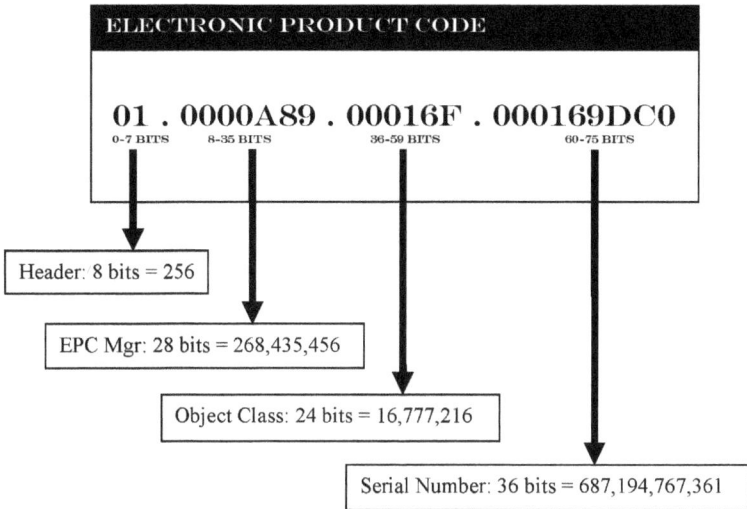

ELECTRONIC PRODUCT CODE

01 . 0000A89 . 00016F . 000169DC0
0-7 BITS   8-35 BITS   36-59 BITS   60-75 BITS

Header: 8 bits = 256

EPC Mgr: 28 bits = 268,435,456

Object Class: 24 bits = 16,777,216

Serial Number: 36 bits = 687,194,767,361

Figure 2.12. Anatomy of basic RFID data.

remote antennas with external connections. The RFID reader antenna sends out a radio wave that powers up the antenna on a passive tag and provides the power for the tag to transmit data. Antennas can be controlled by the software and reader and set to gather information in a certain read range. When selecting a reader antenna, there are several issues that the user should consider:

- Polarization
- Type of antenna
- Placement

Table 2.4. Banks of Information for the Unique Identifier[6]

Bank	Information
0	Access password Kill password
1 (3 Fields)	CRC (cyclic redundancy check) Protocol control EPC data
2	Tag identifier (TID)
3	User data

Polarization

Polarization refers to the direction of electromagnetic waves. Antennas for RFID are polarized either linearly or circularly. For linear polarized antennas the tag and antenna must be in alignment for the tag to be read (Figure 2.13a), while with circularly polarized antennas the tag can be placed almost anywhere on the item and still be read (Figure 2.13b). A Slinky toy best illustrates how circular polarization works. The signal comes out of the antenna in a continuous spiral pattern; however, because of the circular motion, some power is lost with circular antennas.

Types of Antennas

A monostatic antenna is the most frequently used. When using a monostatic antenna, a single antenna functions for both sending and receiving the signal. The monostatic antenna requires only one connector on the reader. When using bistatic antennas, two are required as well as two connectors. One antenna receives transmissions through one connection while the other antenna sends the transmission through the second port.[7]

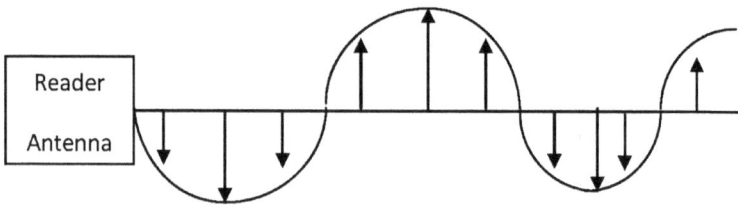

Figure 2.13a. Linear polarization.

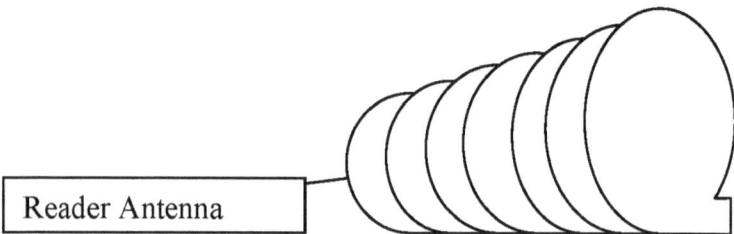

Figure 2.13b. Circular polarization.

Antenna Placement

Antenna and tag placement are closely related. For example, if you choose to use linearly polarized antennas and the signal is only emitted in one direction, then the antenna must be in alignment with the antenna on the tag, as seen in Figure 2.13a. Another issue for any type of antenna is the shadowing effect sometimes seen in a dense tag environment. As previously mentioned, shadowing occurs when a passive tag is not activated because other tags are stacked on top of each other, preventing the antenna from receiving the signal to power up the tag. For example, T-shirts may be stacked on top of one another in a case. The tags could be stacked one on top of the other, causing the top tag to shadow the bottom tag. As previously stated, some readers are made to work better in a dense environment thus eliminating some of the potential for shadowing.

Standards and Regulations

The major obstacle for RFID usage in supply chains today is the need for a set of open global standards.[8] Interoperability between countries with different standards makes it a necessity to have an open set of standards for RFID to reach its full potential, especially in supply chain management.[9] Specifically, issues of tags, frequencies, communication equipment, middleware, and databases all need to be addressed by a global standard. The issue with tags alone is an enormous obstacle. RFID tags differ from one manufacturer to the next and from one application to the next in many ways. For example, inventory management in the apparel industry requires a tag that will operate in a dense environment, whereas inventory management for the pharmaceutical industry requires tags that can be read at short distances. The tags for each of these uses do not necessarily vary in terms of microchips, but they do vary in length of the antenna. Standards are needed not only in individual industries but also across all industries so that the information provided by the use of RFID can benefit organizations across industries, through supply chains, and globally. The biggest issue discussed earlier is the varying frequencies used globally. Each region currently has a different governing body. In the United States the regulatory body is the Federal Communications Commission (FCC), while Europe is governed by the European

Telecommunications Standards Institute (ETSI).[10] Varying governing bodies in each nation or region has made RFID difficult to standardize. Research in RFID is focused on the development of tags that can be read on the varying frequencies.

An auto identification center (Auto-ID Center) at MIT was set up in 1999 to develop the EPC. The Auto-ID Center wanted an RFID system to be based on open standards so that products and materials could be tracked from one country to another.[11] In 2003 the Auto-ID Center passed on the responsibility of developing an open standard to EPC Global, an organization set up as a joint venture by two standards organizations, GS1 International and GS1 U.S. (Uniform Code Council). EPC Global developed a second-generation tag protocol that could be fast-tracked within the International Organization for Standardization (ISO).[12]

The ISO has taken on the task of developing international standards for RFID. For example, ISO 11784 defines the structure of the information on an RFID tag (Figure 2.11), while ISO 11785 defines air interface protocol. The ISO has also developed ISO 18000, which are the standards for automatic identification and item management.[13] ISO 18000 is a set of global standards for air interface. These standards will hopefully create an environment in which frequency for UHF passive tags will no longer be an issue and visibility as products move from one country to another will become commonplace. A list of the current standards is included in the appendix.

CHAPTER 3

Uses of RFID Technology

Imagine having the ability to know where your raw materials are and when they will arrive or where your product is in the distribution channel on a near real-time basis. RFID can be integrated with enterprise resource planning (ERP), supply chain management, and warehouse management systems (WMS) to create a real-time information system so that decisions can be made based on information that is a few seconds or minutes old rather than hours or days old. RFID provides many companies with this ability. However, RFID can benefit organizations internally in many other ways. Simply do a search on RFID using Google or Bing and a multitude of uses will result. As with any technology that is deemed new, there is much skepticism and reluctance to adopt the technology until it has been fully vetted. Most companies don't want to be the early adopters because of the issues they may encounter in getting the technology to function as promised. RFID is not a new technology—it has been around since before World War II—but many of its current uses are new. The technology's capabilities, extreme adaptability, and versatility allow for unique solutions to some problems. There are a multitude of RFID systems for various uses and operating environments (Figure 3.1). RFID, when properly employed, can help companies gain a competitive advantage over their competition.

RFID technology is seen as a method to increase efficiencies in organizations by improving accuracy. Accuracy can be improved in terms of ensuring that customers receive what they order or that the company delivers exactly what customers want in a final product.[1] RFID provides the same capabilities as bar codes but also provides capabilities that are impossible with bar codes alone. For example, RFID does not require line of sight for reading, so there is a time reduction for employees because they do not have to move the package around to find the bar code. As

| Impinj Speedway Reader | Alien 9900 Reader | Omron Reader |

| Alien 9650 Reader | Intermec CN30 Handheld Computer & IP30 Reader | Atid Handheld Reader |

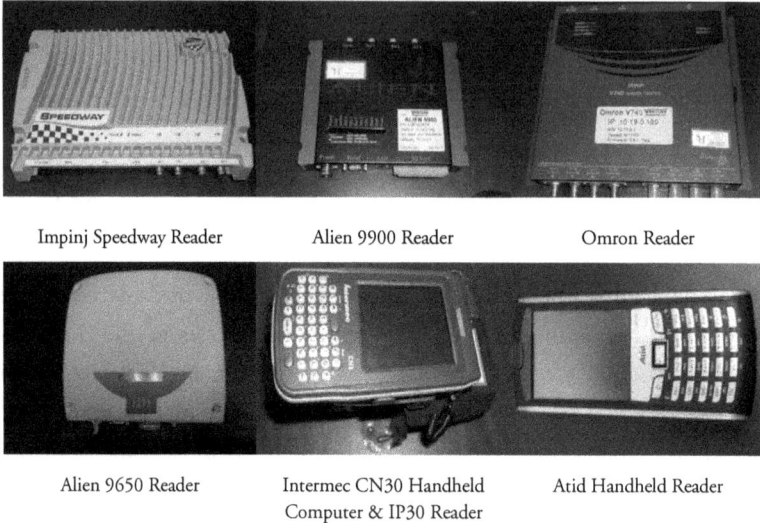

Figure 3.1. Examples of UHF passive RFID readers.

Photographs courtesy of the Sower Business Technology Laboratory, College of Business Administration, Sam Houston State University.

with bar codes, RFID can be used at the item level to uniquely identify the individual item. Product authentication is possible to ensure the product is exactly what it is supposed to be. There are also many advantages to RFID, including its ability to increase traceability, which allows for easier recalls of defective or dangerous items when necessary. Another advantage is greater visibility of product throughout the supply chain.[2]

The National Institute of Standards and Technology (NIST) defines eight nonmutually exclusive types of RFID applications. These applications are explained in the following paragraphs and will be used to categorize current and future uses. The discussion in this chapter will help readers uncover ways the technology may be able to improve the performance of their organizations.

RFID asset management is the ability "to manage inventory of any item that can be tagged"[3] using readers at a fixed location. Applications in this category include electronic article surveillance, which is used to account for items in a retail setting and for record tracking. This application of RFID is also the basis for smart shelves that automatically maintain continuous inventories of tagged items and automatically initiate reordering when stocks reach a specified level.

RFID asset tracking differs from asset management in that multiple readers at multiple locations are incorporated into a central network that "can aggregate and correlate information from each of the readers."[4] This enables the determination of the location of an item in a suitably RFID reader–equipped environment. Asset tracking applications include tracking of containers within production facilities, employees within workplaces, and athletes during sporting events.

RFID authenticity verification is a process or system that can provide evidence of the source of an item and is usually incorporated into a tracking application. A record is created at the beginning of the process and the record can be stored on the tag or in a database. As the tagged item moves through the process or system, it can be determined if the item originated from the correct source. Typically the systems will incorporate cryptography and other methods to prevent the possibility of a clone being used. Digital signatures can be used to verify the authenticity of the item. The pharmaceutical industry uses RFID authenticity verification to control for counterfeit drugs.[5]

RFID matching is an application that matches two or more tagged items together. If the tagged items are not a match, an output device, such as a light or a sound, will be triggered, indicating that there is not a match between the items. RFID matching is widely used in maternity wards, where tags are placed on the mothers and newborns to indicate that they belong together. Another application is to ensure that the right patient receives the right medication by tagging both the patient and the medication.[6]

RFID process control is a process that allows customized action to be taken depending on the information associated with the RFID tag. These processes will facilitate customization of products in manufacturing processes by allowing the RFID tag to tell the process what actions are required for specific products. Sensors also can be integrated with the RFID tags to measure environmental factors, such as humidity, temperature, and air pressure, to indicate whether the tagged item is still usable.[7]

RFID access control systems are used to permit physical access to a facility or an information system to authorized personnel only. Individuals that are authorized to have access usually carry RFID smart cards, sometimes referred to as electronic keys. These RFID smart cards can also be combined with passwords, personal identification numbers, or biometrics to add another layer of security. RFID access control systems can also automatically maintain the dates and times access is permitted for all users. RFID access control is also being used in automobile key applications in two primary ways. The first is a tag or chip imbedded in the traditional automobile key, and the second is a keyless push-button starting system in which the driver must have the appropriate key fob for the vehicle. Once the appropriate key fob is detected, the driver can simply push a button to start the vehicle.[8]

RFID automated payment systems facilitate financial transactions such as toll payments, mass transit fares, and retail payments. The advantages of RFID automated payment are speed and convenience because there is no physical exchange of cash or cards with clerks or machines. These types of systems are a specialized form of access control systems. As such they may require additional security to protect users from fraud and abuse. Resorts and cruise ships are utilizing these systems to link the customers' credit card accounts to them to enable easy payment for meals and purchases in gift shops.[9]

RFID supply chain management systems involve monitoring and controlling raw materials and products from manufacturing to retail sale. Typically there are several applications bundled together, such as asset management, tracking, process control, and payment systems. These systems span multiple organizations, meaning that the RFID systems utilized must be interoperable with other systems in other organizations. These types of systems are referred to as open systems. Open systems are much more vulnerable to unauthorized access and fraud than the closed systems previously discussed. The advantage of an RFID supply chain management system is that it can record information at virtually every stage in the supply chain. In addition, products can be accurately tracked throughout their life cycles. Speed and accuracy of ordering, invoicing, and payment can be realized, as well as reduced supply shortages and stockouts, lower inventory levels, and reduced product loss or theft. Bottlenecks can be identified, recalls can be achieved more easily, and new forms of market research can be utilized.[10]

Current Applications

Current applications of RFID technology reach across many different industries and are used for various purposes. The real advantages of the technology are the flexibility and adaptability that it gives organizations. This chapter contains examples of current and future applications in a number of areas of an organization or supply chain. These examples are adaptable for almost any industry or can in some way be modified for other scenarios. In addition, the ease of integration of RFID with other technologies makes it a viable candidate for many solutions.

RFID Asset Management

RFID asset management is growing in use in many different industries. For example, Sumitomo Electric Lightwave, a company that manufactures fiber-optic cables, has increased productivity through the use of RFID in managing their raw materials inventory. Additionally, by tagging their inventory they have been able to monitor their work-in-progress inventory (WIP) to avoid running out of needed materials.[11]

Another way of utilizing RFID for asset management is to integrate the technology with other technologies, creating greater visibility in both operations and supply chain management. For example, four companies in South Korea selling books and/or health products have pick-to-light paperless order picking and fulfillment systems that have been enhanced by employing RFID. They have been able to increase efficiency and cut costs by reducing errors in their order-fulfillment processes.[12]

RFID asset management can also help organizations to control losses and reduce costs. A tool to help in this effort is the smart shelf. Smart shelves are being used in a number of ways in the pharmaceutical and retail industries. A maternity clothing supplier, Tomorrow's Mother, is monitoring and managing their inventory to prevent inventory problems.[13] By monitoring which items are leaving the shelves and matching those items at the point of sale, the company can keep inventory on the sales floor, increasing the opportunity for potential sales. The information allows employees to monitor items that may be left in dressing rooms as well. In addition, as the items are processed at the point of sale, the inventory is automatically decreased and more can be ordered or brought out of inventory storage. This use also increases customer responsiveness because employees can always know what is in inventory and in what sizes.

RFID asset management, RFID asset tracking, and RFID matching can be useful in many different capacities. For example, loss control is a concern for any airport. Lisbon Airport is using an RFID baggage system to reduce the loss of passenger luggage and to increase the workers' ability to get luggage transferred in a timely manner. Reports indicate that workers at the Lisbon Airport have been able to reduce the time for transferring luggage by 66%.[14] This reduction in time means that luggage is most likely getting on the correct flight with the correct passenger, resulting in fewer losses, lower costs for the airlines and airport, and increased customer satisfaction. In today's high-security environment, luggage is not supposed to board a plane without the passenger who checked it. RFID allows airport employees to match the luggage to the passengers on the flight list, making it easier to comply with that policy.

RFID Asset Tracking

The uses for RFID asset tracking and security are easy to understand and visualize. For example, the oil and gas industry tracks high-value equipment in harsh environments. One of the issues in the past has been the robustness of the tags in harsh environments. One company has designed RFID tags that will survive pressures of 20,000 psi, temperatures of 360 degrees, and high-corrosion environments that may be encountered on offshore drilling platforms.[15] Tagging the oil-field equipment allows the company to track assets as they move from well sites to other areas. As a result, the identification process dramatically decreases the time needed to process the equipment in and out of the field.[16] Once the assets are tagged and tracked in the oil-field environment, the use of the information can be extended by incorporating maintenance management and logs as well.[17] In addition, the use of RFID asset tracking in the oil-field industry decreases waste incurred in terms of idle employees. For example, equipment en route to a drilling site can be monitored during transport which can help pinpoint the time of arrival. This reduces the need for employees to stand around for hours waiting for the equipment so that it can be off-loaded. This should result in an increase in employee productivity.

Hospitals are using RFID to help reduce the loss of assets and also to reduce potential liability for the hospital and doctors. For example, hospitals are using RFID to control operating room assets, reducing the potential for foreign items being left inside of patients when sutured. An executive noted that since the implementation of an RFID system, the facility has experienced time savings, increased productivity, and zero loss of tagged assets, reducing the need for purchasing unnecessary replacements.[18] Although the hospital did not identify any decrease in lawsuits, the potential for that reduction is evident.

Sometimes there is a need to track and control access to high-value documents. One organization found that by tracking documents, they were able to reduce time spent trying to locate files from 4 days to 4 hours because RFID technology reduced human error and increased accuracy and security of the documents. A properly implemented RFID system can establish a tracking system when security badges for employees are equipped with RFID as well so that RFID-equipped files can be matched in a database with the employee who had the item in his or her possession. Another way to accomplish the tracking of high-value documents would be to establish choke points within the physical location.[19] A choke point is an RFID equipped location, such as a portal, that all personnel, equipment, or inventory passes through. This method, however, would require more of an investment in hardware to create the choke points.

RFID asset tracking has proven a success for a manufacturer of tortillas. The tortilla company uses plastic containers to ship the packaged products. The containers are loaded onto independent distributors' vehicles for delivery. The plastic containers are supposed to be returned to the tortilla producer's facility for reuse. However, the producer discovered that they were highly unlikely to ever see the plastic containers again once they left their facility, so they implemented the use of a new container equipped with an RFID tag. This system enabled the tortilla company to locate the containers to ensure they were returned for reuse. As a result, the company is much "greener" because they are not constantly replacing the containers, resulting in a better public image. In addition, they saved over $700,000 in packaging costs, which went to the bottom line as increased profits.[20]

The inability to trace components and products is at the core of all recall problems due to the inability to identify where the items came from and where they are currently. RFID asset tracking creates an environment that allows for traceability throughout the supply chain by adding the ability to trace products from the raw materials that were inputs through to the final sale of the product to the end user. RFID asset tracking also provides the user with a way to trace the defective product back through the supply chain in order to identify the point at which the defect occurred. This type of system allows defective products to be quickly pulled from the shelves so that harm can be minimized and ultimately reduces the potential financial liability the company may face.[21]

RFID asset tracking and RFID asset management can also increase profitability. For example, companies using pallets to ship their product face the possibility of a double loss. The double loss would occur because the company loses both the pallets used to ship the product as well as the product itself. RFID asset management is being used to reduce that loss. Misplaced shipments make it impossible to collect payment from customers, reducing cash flow for the organization. Additional loss occurs if the company has to ship replacement products to the customer because of the loss of the first shipment, which also increases shipping costs.

Often, reusable pallets are not returned by customers. Each lost pallet results in the company having to purchase a new pallet. The loss is as high as 30% of total pallets in use, and the unnecessary replacement costs cause an additional decrease in profitability. A Japanese pallet rental company working with Impinj, an RFID company, developed a pallet with a ruggedized RFID tag called the Mighty Tag and equipped their forklifts with readers. As a result of the enhanced ability to track the pallets, the pallet rental company can now provide a way for their customers to reduce potential losses in both shipments and pallets.[22] A group of Australian companies worked together to test a similar solution over a 3-month period. The experiment's result was that an RFID solution provided 100% accuracy, resulting in a totally reliable system in terms of tracking pallets.[23] The group did not track losses of shipments, but the feasibility of reducing those losses as well is evident.

RFID Authenticity Verification

Counterfeit goods are a global problem. Numerous manufacturers are using RFID authenticity verification as an important tool in their anti-counterfeiting efforts.[24] A group of Scandinavian companies placed RFID tags on bottles of medications encoded with the unique serial number and medication's expiration date. As the medication is shipped, the items are scanned with a reader and the destination information is entered into a database. When the product arrives at its destination, it is scanned with a reader, again verifying the authenticity of the medication. If the medication has been switched during transit, the information provided by the RFID system will aid law enforcement in their efforts to find the culprit.[25]

A clothing company has RFID tags sewn into the labels of its garments. The company controls the number of tags sent to its suppliers. Suppliers making more than the number of garments ordered from them will be easily identifiable. This gives the clothing company the ability to find out who the bad suppliers are and to quit sending them business.[26]

The Wynn Las Vegas was the first casino to begin using RFID tags in its casino chips. Since that first implementation, RFID-enabled chips have become the industry norm. In December 2010 at 3:50 a.m., the Bellagio (MGM) hotel-casino was robbed, and the thief made off with $1.5 million in RFID-enabled chips. By 3:51 a.m. the chips were electronically disabled, making them totally worthless to the thief. The casinos are using the information from the RFID system in multiple ways. The first is verifying the origin of the chip, the second is to control theft, and the third is to track guest behavior. RFID-enabled chips allow casinos to track the time guests have been playing, the games they like, the types of drinks they order, and their average bets. This information allows the casino to be more responsive to customer needs.[27]

The biggest threat to the ticketing industry is counterfeiting. As a result, event managers are using RFID authenticity verification. The Olympic games in China had 7 million event tickets available for sale. Each one of these tickets had RFID-embedded tags to reduce the incidence of pirated tickets and speed up the event entry process. The tickets were quite successful because they were too difficult to replicate.[28] RFID-tag-equipped wristbands are also used in authenticity verification. The South by Southwest Festival is an annual event held in Austin, Texas, that draws approximately 23,000 people. Each person is given a wristband with an RFID chip embedded. The event coordinators use output devices to indicate whether the wristband is authentic or not. As a result of this process, counterfeit wristbands were completely eliminated.[29]

RFID Matching

RFID matching is currently being used in security and asset and materials tracking. The health care industry is using the matching concept in many different ways. Over the past few years, we have all seen the headlines about infants being taken out of hospital maternity wards by unauthorized people. Some maternity wards are now using RFID systems to increase security by placing an RFID-tag-equipped band around the baby's ankle that will sound an alarm if it is removed without the proper tools and authorization. An RFID-tag-equipped wristband is placed on the parents, and then the baby's and the parents' bands are linked to each other in a database. When the infant is taken past a certain point in the maternity ward and there is not a matching wristband with the infant, an alarm will sound, alerting everyone in the area. In addition, the technology can alert medical staff when the mother and infant are leaving the ward before being properly discharged.[30]

The health care industry is also using RFID matching to tie employees and patients to medications. For example, a smart shelf can be used to tie the drug to the individual removing it from inventory by tagging the bottles with RFID and then having employee identification cards equipped with RFID tags. This allows for the drug and the employee to be associated in a database. In addition, a similar approach is used in hospitals and nursing homes when drugs are dispensed to patients. When the employee removes the drugs from the smart shelf, that action is recorded by the system. The patient has a wristband, and the information for the medication that person is supposed to be given is recorded in a database. When the employee delivers the medication to the patient, both the tag on the medication and the tag on the patient are read. If the medication was taken from the wrong bottle, an alarm or a code will come up indicating that the employee is about to administer the wrong medication. This application has significantly reduced the number of incidents of patients being given the wrong medication.

Another interesting use of the matching concept is the integration of vending machines with RFID. Cribmaster is offering an RFID vending system for managing tools in a tool crib. The technology automatically ties workers to the tools that they are withdrawing from the tool crib. This application allows employers to track which employees have certain tools and enables them to track down lost tools by tracing the jobs that the employee was assigned.

Waste management is an industry in which RFID matching is proving extremely useful. The manufacturers embed RFID tags in the waste carts

and the trucks are equipped with an RFID reader and a computer to identify where the truck is when it picks up the waste. This system allows the
waste management company to trace the origin of the waste for billing purposes and avoid double collection to reduce costs. In addition, the system
allows for proof of when the truck made its rounds, which helps in cases
where customers forget to put out their waste but claim the truck didn't
come by and helps determine if the customer is putting out more waste than
is allowed, and helps the company to keep track of the costly carts.[31]

RFID Process Control

RFID process control can be seen in many forms. For example, Coca-
Cola is revolutionizing the vending machine industry with the Freestyle
vending machine. The new vending machine allows for more variety by
offering more than 100 drink selections in the same space as a regular
vending machine by integrating RFID in the mixing process. The Freestyle vending machine allows Coca-Cola to be more customer responsive
by tracking the most popular drinks. The data information systems automatically track the flavor cartridges through a combination of sensors
and RFID. In addition, the company is able to track customer information, resulting in better marketing to the consumer.[32]

The oil industry is also using RFID process control technology. For
example, Marathon Oil Company has incorporated RFID into their
downhole drilling process by fitting the downhole tools with RFID to
actuate well-borne equipment.[33] Further, Marathon Oil is developing
two new RFID applications. "Type 1" applications use the RFID tag by
placing it on the casing string. The reader can then send the signal for a
different operation when the equipment reaches a specific downhole location. "Type II" applications use downhole tools that are configured with a
reader and the tool will work when the correct code is received. Marathon
Oil Company estimated that these uses of RFID would result in a savings
of $17 million annually and improve operational safety for their employ-
ees.[34] Marathon Oil Company has adapted RFID systems to open and
close cementing stage collars and for many other processes as well.[35]

RFID process control can help organizations develop new cost-saving
processes. For example, a hotel in Vancouver tracks linens through the
laundry using RFID. The hotel's original intent was to track the quality

of the laundry service to make sure that the linens were clean when they were reused. The hotel found that while they achieved the desired result of tracking, there were other cost-saving results because employees no longer had to count the linens overnight by hand. Hotel management feels that it will be difficult to track return on investment (ROI), but nonetheless, they see the implementation of the RFID process control system as a profitable investment.[36]

RFID Access Control

RFID access control is fast becoming a staple of the security industry; however, many of the utilizations have been expanded in recent years. As discussed in chapter 1, parking lots and garages are carrying the use of the technology one step further to include improved customer service. The use of RFID in the security industry is more far-reaching than access and payment control for parking facilities. For example, ADT is using proximity high frequency (HF) RFID to reduce false alarms in its home security systems (Figure 3.2). According to ADT, most false alarms originate because of mistakes made at the keypad. They are offering wireless

Figure 3.2. RFID controlled access system. RFID reader, keypad, identification cards, and keyfob.

Photograph courtesy of the Sower Business Technology Laboratory, College of Business Administration, Sam Houston State University.

key fobs to activate and deactivate systems remotely, which minimizes the potential for mistakes at the keypad.[37]

According to Tom Ridge, the first secretary of the U.S. Department of Homeland Security, "That's one of the beautiful things about RFID. It's another security measure embedded in the U.S. economy."[38] The Department of Homeland Security is using RFID tags to track visitors' border crossings, increasing the ability to match entries and exits in a timely manner without slowing down the process for all travelers.[39] The State Department is now issuing passports in the United States with embedded RFID tags. There are a number of states that are issuing driver's licenses and car tags with RFID tags embedded. There are several security issues currently emerging as a result of these trials. One issue arises in the delivery of renewed driver's license and car tags. While in transit to the recipient, the RFID tags can be read by anyone with a reader. However, encryption technology coupled with RFID technology is a viable solution to the issue.

Low frequency (LF) RFID tags are increasingly replacing magnetic stripes on cards used for access control. One example is the use of RFID tags in room keycards in hotels and rental units. The tags are programmed at check-in just as the old magnetic keycards were and provide guests access to their rooms, the gym, the pool, and other guest facilities. Because the cards must be very close to the antenna in order to be read, the risk of someone "stealing" the access code programmed on the tag is very low, so shielded cases are not necessary.

Another example of RFID access control is the use of RFID tags for frequent users of airport parking facilities, as mentioned in the opening chapter of this book. Regular customers may register and be issued identification cards with LF RFID tags. Upon entry into the lot, the customer places the card against the reader and is immediately identified by the system. The customer may be greeted by name by the parking attendant. Frequent-user premium points serve as an incentive and are automatically tracked by the system. A benefit of this system is that it increases efficiency of the arrival and departure process. Paper parking passes that are date stamped are no longer necessary with this system. The customer simply scans the card upon checkout, the bill is automatically presented, and the customer may pay the bill with a credit card—all without an attendant being present.

RFID access control is also being used in the pharmaceutical industry. For example, secure-locking smart cabinets that combine ultra high frequency (UHF) and HF RFID technology help ensure inventory accuracy, verify that the correct product is being used, and also control access to the medication to ensure that only authorized employees have access. Additionally, the cabinet, when coupled with middleware and ERP software, creates a near real-time information system, allowing companies using the technology to make decisions based on the most current information available.

A current trend for education is equipping school buses with RFID technology and then issuing RFID-embedded identification cards to students. This type of system allows the bus driver to verify that every student on that bus is on the correct bus. In addition, the time of arrival of the student on the bus and whether that student rode the bus to school can be accurately tracked. This RFID matching process also allows the bus driver to ensure that students are not left behind at school, adding another element of RFID access control. Buses can be equipped to verify that all students on the bus have departed, preventing students from being left on buses at the end of the routes.

In October 2010, a 4-year-old prekindergarten student was inadvertently left alone on a parked school bus in a Texas school district.[40] The driver was charged with endangering a child for not checking the bus thoroughly before parking it. Two other school districts in Texas are piloting a system that uses RFID tags in the student identification badges.[41] Currently the system is used primarily to track students while they are on campus; however, strategically placed readers on school buses in the district could be used to ensure that the bus is empty at the end of the day. This system could have prevented the pre-K student's endangerment had it been deployed in the school bus where this incident occurred.

Monitoring students using RFID technologies faces some opposition from parents and the American Civil Liberties Union, who fear the technology exposes students to possible identity theft and stalking. In 2005, a California school district dismantled its RFID pilot program because of these parental concerns.[42] These concerns will have to be effectively addressed before we can expect to see widespread use of RFID systems to track students while they are at school and on school buses.

The health care industry can also use RFID verification to track and verify the location of Alzheimer's patients. This year, Aetrex has begun marketing shoes with embedded active RFID tags with global positioning system (GPS) capability for use by Alzheimer's patients.[43] Shoes were chosen as the best place to implant the tags because almost all Alzheimer's patients who wander off remember to wear their shoes. Tracking is provided by GPSShoe.com for a monthly connection fee in addition to the initial cost of the shoes. This usage will likely grow as more and more baby boomers reach the age where Alzheimer's typically occurs. This usage of RFID is likely to be subject to the same concerns as its use within public schools.

RFID Automated Payment

Vending machines are being equipped to use RFID as a cashless payment system. This use of the technology is being extended into self-service laundries and kiosks.[44] The use of RFID as a means of paying for vending machine purchases began in the United States in the mid-2000s. Acceptance and widespread utilization of this application have been severely limited by the slow pace of the use of RFID tags in credit and debit cards in the United States. Europe has, for the most part, abandoned magnetic stripes and embraced a sister technology to RFID, the Europay Master-Card Visa (EMV) smart card and personal identification number (PIN) technology, discussed in chapter 5, for credit cards. The United States has been slow to embrace this technology, resulting in very slow development of RFID enabled commercial vending machines. However, there have been some notable successes.

RFID has taken automated vending out of the box, according to Ray Friedrich, president of Fast Track Convenience, a division of Sterling Service, a food service management company, and a 20-year veteran of the vending machine business: "We can offer deli-fresh food and products in any color, shape or size."[45]

Fast Track Convenience teamed up with Freedom Shopping to create a self-service RFID kiosk for the food service market. They discovered that they were the first. "The conventional wisdom is that item-level tracking with RFID is ten years away," says Rob Simmons, cofounder of Freedom Shopping. "We've been doing this for two years, with a strong return on investment. . . . The only practical way to do an unmanned application like this is to use RFID," says Simmons. "We were new to RFID, and had heard that you couldn't tag metals and liquids and you couldn't do item-level tagging profitably. But that wasn't true." Today, the

Freedom Shopping System is in production at more than 20 minimarts across the United States, including five customers of Fast Track Convenience in the Detroit area. One customer's sales have increased threefold and profits per item more than doubled since the introduction of the RFID kiosk.[46]

RFID Supply Chain Management

RFID supply chain management has the potential to increase efficiency, accuracy, and security of the processes by improving information sharing within the supply chain.[47] The cost of implementation and lack of standards are the two biggest issues facing this use of the RFID technology. Benefits of using RFID supply chain management include reduced stockouts, improved asset visibility, real-time decision-making capabilities, improved reverse logistics, counterfeit prevention, and prevention of obsolescence.[48] The two most notable entities leading the initiative in RFID supply chain management are Walmart and the Department of Defense (DOD).[49] There have been challenges for both Walmart and the DOD in implementing RFID throughout their supply chains. Walmart has had many stumbling blocks, but the most notable is the fact that most of their smaller suppliers have not been able to realize a return on their RFID investment. In other words, the supplier may simply see RFID as a cost of doing business with a company such as Walmart and never see the full potential that the technology can provide to their organization because it is still somewhat cost prohibitive for the supplier to add readers and other equipment necessary for uses beyond simple compliance with the Walmart directive to apply tags to their products. Larger companies that are suppliers to Walmart have been able to see a return on their investment. Procter & Gamble Company found significant benefits in helping streamline processes, shipping, and speeding the movement of their products to distribution centers.[50]

The DOD is using RFID supply chain management to track and maintain the security of shipments entering the war zones of Iraq and Afghanistan. The military was able to reduce theft by monitoring the containers as they move from the port to the troops.[51] The result of the DOD's implementation of RFID is a development of policies and guidelines for supply chain implementation. The DOD has not been able to calculate an ROI because it does not collect information on both the cost and the benefits that are associated with the implementation of RFID technology.

In addition to the efforts made by Walmart and the DOD, Canada is using RFID in the country's food-supply chain in an effort to guarantee food safety. Food is tracked through user-defined routes, and any deviation from the expected times and conditions will cause an alert to be sent to process owners. This system also allows for traceability in the event of contaminated food reaching the market.[52]

The opportunities for RFID supply chain management are endless and systems continue to evolve. The integration of RFID with ERP software will present a multitude of opportunities for organizations using this technology. However, cost is still the main issue in implementing RFID systems on the scale of supply chains.[53] With the introduction of UHF passive tags with longer read ranges the cost should begin to come down. In the beginning of an RFID supply chain management implementation, the central organization that is pushing the initiative will continue to see smaller companies in the supply chain maintaining a slap-and-ship approach, applying RFID tags as required by the customer but without realizing any of the internal benefits of RFID. For those smaller companies, they may continue to see RFID as just a cost of doing business with their customer.

Integrating RFID With Other Technologies

RFID systems are often integrated with other technologies beyond just a database. The following sections discuss some frequently encountered types of integration and their applications. This is by no means an exhaustive list because new and innovative integration applications appear nearly every day. Rather this discussion provides examples of a variety of applications in various environments and also background to stimulate ideas for potential new integration applications.

Enterprise Resource Planning (ERP) and RFID

The combination of RFID's ability to provide near real-time information and an ERP software system's ability to quickly process that data, integrate it, and make it available across the organization sounds like a marriage made in heaven. Many ERP systems providers, including SAP and JD Edwards, have developed RFID integration capabilities for their ERP systems, but it has had a somewhat rocky start since its inception in 2004.

A key early motivator for the integration of RFID with ERP systems was Walmart's decision to require its suppliers to provide RFID-tagged products by 2007. An early entry into the RFID-ERP integration technology arena was SAP with the introduction of its packaged RFID-solution system using a middleware system called Auto-ID, which interfaced with SAP's R/3 ERP system. This system was specifically designed to enable suppliers to become Walmart compliant and therefore focused mainly on passive RFID tag systems.[54] However, as of 2008, widespread adoption of this system was delayed by "problems with data filtering and analysis, clunky tag-read work-arounds, continuing high costs, and unrealized returns on investment."[55] Until recently, lack of standardization has also been a problem that has inhibited integration of RFID with ERP. These problems led many organizations to utilize a stand-alone database system to support RFID rather than integrate it with their ERP systems.

Some users have employed mobile phones as RFID readers for an auto-ID system. The goods can be scanned via a mobile phone that is coupled with a cross-talk agent. The cross-talk agent submits the data to a cross-talk server, which injects the data into the SAP R/3 auto-ID infrastructure.[56]

Bar Code Technology and RFID

RFID, while more expensive, has significant advantages over bar codes—and the cost differential is rapidly narrowing.

- RFID tags do not require line of sight in order to be read, and, depending on the type of tag, can be read at greater distances.
- RFID tags can also be read so much faster than bar codes that it appears that all tags in a center are read simultaneously rather than sequentially as with bar codes.
- RFID has read/write capability, which bar codes lack.
- RFID tags are more durable than bar codes and may be implanted within products, ensuring long-term traceability.

- Active RFID can be more readily integrated with sensor technologies, such as GPS and environmental monitoring, to facilitate remote, near real-time monitoring of shipments, components, and materials.

These advantages facilitate an organization's ability to provide timely information required for agile performance. As Mark Roberti, editor of *RFID Journal* put it:

> Saying bar codes are cheaper than RFID tags is like saying a wood-handled hammer is cheaper than a nail gun. Well, yeah. But it takes a mere fraction of the time to finish a job with a nail gun than it would with an old-fashioned hammer. Similarly, apparel retailers have found that it takes 75 percent to 80 percent less time to complete a store inventory with RFID than with bar codes.[57]

RFID is often integrated with bar codes. Some RFID tags are also printed with bar codes. This facilitates the reading of essential information by existing bar code technology while providing the advantages associated with the use of RFID technology. For example, Case Study 6.3 documents CHEP's use of both RFID and bar code technologies to track shipment, receipt, inspection, and repair of reusable containers. The bar-coded labels are applied to the exposed external sides of the containers to enable operators to visually differentiate tagged containers from those not tagged. The RFID tags are applied to the bottom of the container and provide a unique identifier, which enables remote tracking of the container through all phases of the process using handheld and fixed-position readers.

Sensors and RFID

A variety of sensors can be integrated with RFID technology to detect and report on a variety of parameters; however, sensor tags have been somewhat slow to come into widespread use, largely because they cost more than standard RFID tags. One application is to combine RFID with a temperature sensor on perishable packages to indicate more accurately when shelf life has expired. Richard MacManus predicts that "chemical-biological sensors may be used to monitor food supply and food recalls, together with temperature and other sensors."[58]

The U.S. military has, for a number of years, used active RFID sensor technology in its logistics system. For example, the U.S. Army uses active RFID tags and a variety of sensors to monitor temperature, shock, unauthorized entry, and a variety of other critical parameters for shipments to war zones.[59] As early as 2004, the U.S. Navy was testing an active RFID sensor network to monitor temperature, humidity, and atmospheric pressure in containers used to store aircraft parts.[60] The Navy had experienced instances where expensive parts had been damaged due to environmental problems and found the RFID sensor network could provide a relatively low-cost approach to monitoring the environmental condition of its stored parts inventory.

Because sensor applications frequently require the RFID system to operate in harsh environments, UHF RFID tags have been developed utilizing a dual antenna configuration to minimize blockage of the signal due to the presence of liquids or metals. Continued technological development of smaller and more durable sensors/tags will increase the use of RFID integration with sensors for the purpose of remote monitoring of areas and assets.

Robotics and RFID

For a number of years, leading companies with sophisticated computer numerically controlled (CNC) manufacturing technologies have used "smart products" that tell the CNC machines how to process them as they move from workstation to workstation. Until recently, this has been accomplished using bar codes. Now many organizations have begun using RFID tags instead of barcodes, largely because RFID does not require line of sight and RFID tags can be read faster than bar codes, which increases the efficiency of the processes.

During the past 5 years, researchers have envisioned many opportunities for RFID-guided robots, from helping families tend to disabled relatives and guiding vision-impaired shoppers in retail stores to automating the taking of physical inventories (Figure 3.3).[61]

In 2010, a research team at Georgia Tech announced the development of prototypes of personal robots for health care applications. They addressed the challenge of how to enable the robot to "perceive, manipulate and understand the world around it so it can interact with humans and objects to perform specific tasks—like loading a dishwasher or delivering medicine"[62] through the use of passive UHF RFID:

Figure 3.3. R-Bot: A prototype automated inventory robot.

Photograph courtesy of the Sower Business Technology Laboratory, College of Business
Administration, Sam Houston State University.

Humans and/or objects can be tagged with passive UHF RFID
labels, providing the interface through which a personal robot can
interact to carry out its tasks . . . *"Passive Ultra-High Frequency
(UHF) RFID tags are well matched to robots' needs. Unlike low-
frequency (LF) and high-frequency (HF) RFID tags, passive UHF
RFID tags are readable from across a room, enabling a mobile robot to
efficiently discover and locate them. Because they don't have onboard
batteries to wear out, their lifetime is virtually unlimited. And unlike
bar codes and other visual tags, RFID tags are readable when they're
visually occluded. For less than $0.25 per tag, users can apply self-
adhesive UHF RFID tags throughout their home."*[63]

Global Positioning Systems and RFID

GPS and RFID are sometimes used in combination in order to provide
more complete material tracking capability. RFID has a typical maximum
read distance of about 100 m. GPS does not typically work indoors or in
an environment with tall structures, such as might exist in a large city or

a storage yard, which block the system's line of sight access to satellites. Tall structures sometimes reflect satellite signals, resulting in an incorrect position being reported.

Systems such as the Savi GlobalTag (ST-694) contain an active RFID tag, a satellite modem, and a GPS receiver.

> The GlobalTag includes a Satellite Modem for communications anywhere RFID readers are not available. When RFID infrastructure is not present, the GlobalTag automatically uploads data to RFID networks via satellite. GlobalTag provides GPS location coordinates with every satellite transmission. Unlike other satellite tags, GlobalTag has active RFID functionality, so battery power is not expended on satellite communications when the tag is within range of an active (RFID) reader.[64]

The Global Tag was developed as a joint project with Savi, Numerex, and the U.S. Transportation Command (USTRANSCOM) in response to a DOD "mandate for an asset tag that can be used to track assets . . . the entire time that asset is in the supply chain—from the time it is packed up in a container, loaded onto a ship, unloaded and delivered."[65]

Other RFID/GPS applications include a school bus alert system developed during the mid-2000s. The system uses RFID tags embedded in student ID cards to be sure that students get on the right bus, exit at the correct destination, and are not left on the bus at the end of the day. In addition, a GPS system tracks the bus and alerts parents via a cell phone linkage when the school bus approaches so that students do not have to stand at bus stops for indeterminate periods of time in inclement weather.

Almost 10 years ago, Applied Digital Solutions announced the development of a subdermal, implantable RFID/GPS device for tracking individuals. There was speculation about possible applications for the devices:

> Law enforcement officials could require use of embedded RFID/GPS on parolees as a condition of parole. Stalkers who have court orders placed on them to avoid a celebrity or ex-girlfriend could similarly be tracked. Another really interesting application would be counter-terrorism. Imagine a suspected terrorist having a GPS tracking device secretly implanted.[66]

Of course, there are significant privacy issues associated with the covert use of RFID/GPS tracking devices. In late 2011, the U.S. Supreme Court agreed to hear the appeal of a case involving covert tracking of a suspect by police using such a device attached to the suspect's car. The appeal revolves around Fourth Amendment issues of unreasonable search. As discussed in chapter 4, the widespread use of RFID/GPS for tracking individuals depends on not only the outcome of the legal challenges but also the willingness of the public to accept these applications as appropriate uses of the technology.

Retail Systems and RFID

The possible uses for RFID with retail systems are seemingly endless. IBM, among others, has developed a system that reads RFID tags and customizes in-store or outdoor advertising to fit the customer whose tag has been read. The advantage is that customers will only be presented with advertising for products and services that are relevant to them. According to the Advertising Association, the industry body that represents advertisers, "Outdoor RFID advertising is an exciting prospect for the industry. Ads can be made more relevant to the consumer and it will boost interest in the medium."[67]

The integration of RFID with retail point-of-sale (POS) systems for uses such as improved inventory management to prevent stockouts and automated customer purchasing has been around in some form, from discussion to actual implementation, for a number of years. It is the latter integration—automated customer purchasing—that has been the subject of some controversy. In this application, individual products would be RFID tagged and the customer's cart would be equipped with a reader. As items are added to the cart, a list would be maintained and the customer's RFID-enabled credit or debit card would be charged upon exit from the store—all without the need for a human checker. As has been discussed earlier, RFID-enabled credit and debit cards have been slow to catch on in the United States, largely because of security concerns. However, this application is easily technologically feasible.

Summary

The most challenging issues involving integration of RFID with other technologies are, in many cases, not technological but cultural and legal. This is much less of a problem for industrial uses of the technologies, but is highly significant for consumer uses. This is not a unique situation; many new technologies have had to contend with the same difficulties. Automobiles were legally banned from many areas early in their intro-duction due to the fear that the noise would frighten horses and that the fast-moving vehicles would threaten public safety. We successfully resolved those concerns; we will do the same with RFID.

CHAPTER 4

RFID Is Not a Solution Waiting for a Problem

Humanity is acquiring all the right technology for all the wrong reasons.

R. Buckminster Fuller

Some organizations still look for the *magic bullet* that will solve all their problems without necessitating change on their part. Such a thing has never existed and is unlikely to exist in the future. RFID is a remarkable technology with many important applications in organizations of all kinds, but it is no magic bullet. The actual benefits derived from the use of RFID depend on a number of factors, including proper selection of equipment, proper design and execution of the implementation, and effective integration of the information obtained into the organization's operations and decision-making processes. Another critical success factor is selection of an application for which RFID is the best solution.

According to *NIST Special Publication 800-98*,[1] the following are major advantages of RFID over other automatic identification and data capture (AIDC) technologies such as bar codes:

- RFID does not require optical line of sight for communication.
- RFID can read multiple tags simultaneously rather than sequentially, as with bar codes, providing greater communication speed.
- RFID is capable of communicating over greater distances than optical technologies, such as bar codes.

The following are other advantages listed by the NIST for RFID over other AIDC technologies:

- The capability for rewritable memory
- The ability to interface with environmental sensors
- Enhanced security features

Despite these advantages, there are many applications where RFID may not be the best technology. If simple access control is required, a key works well. But if you also desire to collect information about who accesses the secured areas and when, then RFID is the better option. Bar codes are often the better option for tracking small, low-cost items in a warehouse. RFID would be a better option for large items that would require multiple bar code labels to facilitate reading. Bar coding would probably be a more cost-effective technology than RFID for items presented to the reader sequentially and under controlled conditions, such as on a conveyor belt. RFID is the better option for reading multiple items simultaneously where line of sight is a problem.

Improvement of Supply Chain Effectiveness and Efficiency Through RFID

RFID technology can significantly improve business performance. We have conducted a number of research studies into the uses and benefits of RFID in business organizations. In one study[2] of 122 operations professionals in U.S. manufacturing companies, we found that RFID utilization can directly improve operational performance. However, in another study[3] of the benefits of RFID technology utilization on supply chain performance, utilizing information provided by 155 respondents in both manufacturing and service organizations in the United States, we surprisingly found that the direct effect of RFID utilization on supply chain performance, while nonsignificant, was negative. The study showed that RFID utilization had a positive impact on supply chain information sharing, which in turn had a positive effect on supply chain performance. Upon reflection, these results really make sense. When RFID is implemented solely due to a mandate by a customer or a desire to have the "latest technology" without a good idea of how to leverage that technology, it becomes just an additional cost of doing business and thus negatively affects profitability and performance. However, when RFID is utilized to provide near real-time information, it does improve supply chain performance, as shown in Figure 4.1.

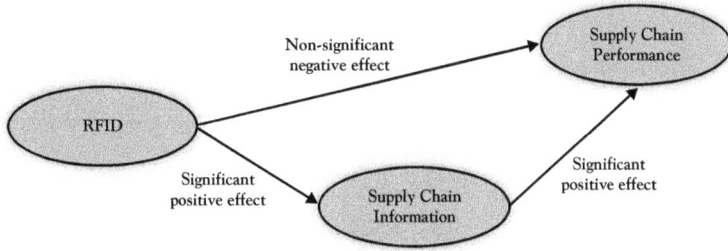

Figure 4.1. RFID effect on supply chain performance.

Our most recent 2011 study[4] of 328 professionals in manufacturing organizations in the United States provided insight into how RFID affects logistics performance. As in the 2010 study, we found that the direct effect of RFID on logistics performance was negative—that is, simply implementing RFID just adds to cost if little use is made of the technology besides retaining current customers who mandate its use. It simply becomes a cost of doing business. However, when RFID's capabilities are utilized to provide more timely information, it increases organizational agility, which in turn increases logistics performance. Agile organizations can respond more quickly to their customers' wants and needs, making them more attractive to the customer. Again, these findings make sense. It is not RFID per se that improves logistics performance, but the utilization of the near real-time information and its sharing with supply chain partners that RFID facilitates that improves logistics performance.

It has been shown that RFID can facilitate the sharing of near real-time information among supply chain partners. The result of this improved information sharing is improved supply chain performance,[5] which means cost savings and efficiency gains. Organizations and supply chains that incorporate RFID technologies appropriately can gain competitive advantage through increased operational and supply chain performance. As businesses strive to gain competitive advantage and market share, RFID technology is increasingly gaining acceptance as an effective approach to doing so.

Automatic Identification Technology and In-Transit Visibility

By USTRANSCOM AIT Project Office

To enhance efficiency, U.S. Transportation Command (USTRANS-COM) was appointed Department of Defense's (DOD) lead proponent for in-transit visibility (ITV). USTRANSCOM was already designated as the lead proponent for automatic information technology (AIT). Since AIT is the leading enabler of ITV, being the proponent for both provides a natural synergy for improving USTRANSCOM's ability to provide forces with actionable logistics information. In close collaboration with Defense Logistics Agency (DLA), USTRANSCOM continues to coordinate the insertion of passive radio frequency identification (pRFID) technology throughout DOD for better supply chain management. This pRFID network automatically receipts for shipments at DLA depots that are instrumented for aRFID. The Air Mobility Command, a component command of USTRANSCOM, has instrumented all their major aerial ports in the continental United States. Experience gained in the US Central Command and other locations with satellite and sensor technology has helped ensure military forces with the ability to provide ITV to austere locations globally. USTRANSCOM's efforts to migrate active RFID legacy read/write

Figure 4.2. C-130 cargo plane.

U.S. Air Force photo by Tech. Sgt. Howard Blair. Public domain.

systems from the current format to one compliant with the International Organization for Standardization (ISO) has progressed rapidly and will be complete by 2012. Further, next generation applications are being looked at for future use throughout DOD for more robust supply chain management.

Myths

Myth 1: RFID Is an Invasion of Privacy

One common myth about RFID relates to its use in personal identification systems. The myth is that the RFID tag used in those systems contains personal information that can be read by anyone with a scanner. This has led to websites suggesting people with identification cards wrap them in aluminum foil to prevent unauthorized scanning. Retailers now sell RFID-shielding wallets, which supposedly prevent unauthorized scanning of RFID-containing materials stored within. The truth revolves around what is actually encoded on the tag, the type of RFID tag used, the purpose of the tag, and the security of the database to which the tag is linked. Some examples of and solutions to these security dimensions are shown in Table 4.1.

Table 4.1. Security Dimensions, Examples, and Solution Options

Dimension	Example	Solutions
Information encoded on tag	• EPC code only • Account number • Personal information	• Restrict type of information encoded • Use additional identifier such as a PIN
Type of tag used	• EMV • LF • HF • UHF	• The RFID-related EMV is as secure as magnetic stripe • Use most restricted read-distance tag practical for application
Purpose of tag	• Part identification • Personal identification • Access control	• Encode only EPC code and tie to secure database • Require additional identifier such as a PIN for access cards
Security of database	• Virtually all RFID applications	• Management controls • Operational controls • Technical controls

What is actually encoded on an RFID tag and how easy is it to extract personal information surreptitiously? In general, the only information contained on a passive RFID tag (the kind generally used in identification systems) is a number as shown in Figure 4.1 and discussed previously in chapter 2 (Figure 2.11). This number does not usually contain any coded information of any kind. Rather it identifies a record in a protected database. Personal information about the holder of the RFID-equipped identification is contained in that database. An analogy can be made to an automobile license tag. Ignoring vanity plates, the number on an automobile license tag contains no information. The tag number identifies a record in a secured database that contains information about the person to whom the tag was issued. In order to obtain personal information from either a license tag or an RFID-enabled identification card, a person would have to obtain the number and then obtain access to the secured database. The security of the personal information in both cases is almost exclusively dependent on the security of the database.

The type of tag used affects the security by affecting the ease with which information may be read from the tag. In general, the greater the read distance, the easier it is to obtain unauthorized access to the data encoded on the tag. Therefore an LF tag would be more secure than either an HF or a UHF tag. The RFID-related Europay MasterCard Visa (EMV) technology provides the greatest security by requiring contact with the reader in order to gain access to the data.

The purpose of the tag also affects security. Tags used to simply identify what they are attached to usually only encode the basic EPC code. This code by itself is usually meaningless. The EPC code is tied to a record in a database where the other, possibly sensitive, information

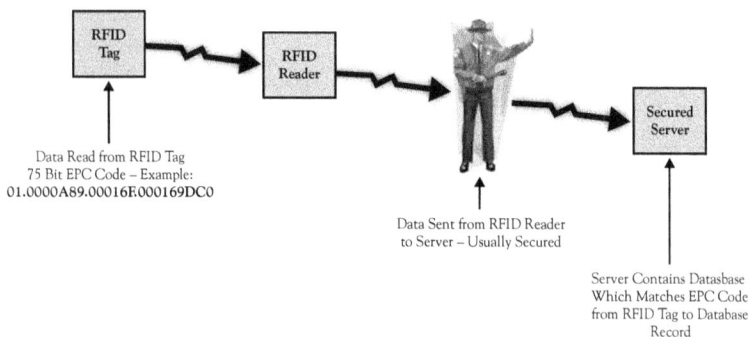

RFID Tag

RFID Reader

Secured Server

Data Read from RFID Tag
75 Bit EPC Code – Example:
01.0000A89.00016F.000169DC0

Data Sent from RFID Reader
to Server – Usually Secured

Server Contains Datasbase
Which Matches EPC Code
from RFID Tag to Database
Record

Figure 4.3. RFID information transfer.

resides. Tags used to control access—for example, keycards—are a different story. These tags function in the same way as keys in a mechanical lock and with no security controls can provide access to whoever has physical possession of the card. A further problem is that someone might access the information from the card and create a clone card that functions just as the original. The same risk of unauthorized access by use of a clone card occurs with magnetic striping technology commonly used on debit and credit cards.

RFID, however, provides an additional capability over automobile license tags or magnetic stripes, which is the ability to track the tag within an RFID reader–enabled environment. For example, a building equipped with a network of RFID readers can track the location of all the RFID tags within that read-equipped facility. In some school districts, student identification cards containing RFID tags enable school districts to take attendance automatically, ensure that students depart on the correct bus, and ensure that all students are evacuated in an emergency. However, as previously mentioned, critics have suggested that these tag-equipped identification cards enable unauthorized access to personal information and student movements. The concerns are so widespread that legislators have become involved. In Texas, House Bill 1134 (2011) was introduced to ensure that parents are fully informed before a school district implements the technology.[6] It remains to be seen if the perception of unnecessary invasion of privacy by some will outweigh the benefits provided by RFID of being able to account for students and help ensure their safety.

There are some current applications involving RFID that do cause concern about the security of sensitive information. Some credit card issuers who are beginning to use RFID tags in conjunction with or in place of the traditional magnetic stripe encode the user's account number, expiration date, and security data on the tag. A relatively inexpensive handheld RFID reader could extract the information, which can be encoded on a clone card. Some card issuers, such as American Express, do not encode the account number on the RFID tag in a way that would enable it to be stolen in this way. Other card issuers change the security code at every transaction, which limits a clone card to one unauthorized transaction. The EMV smart card technology (a technology related to RFID), widely used in Europe, utilizes "multiple layers of security, starting with an

RFID-like tag in each card that stores and transmits encrypted data and a unique identifier that can change with each transaction."[7]

Tags that are incorporated into identification cards for access control purposes (keycards) do not usually contain personal information. However, it is possible to read the information on the tag and create a clone chip that can then permit unauthorized access if the system does not provide additional protections. Dan Mullen, Association for Automatic Identification and Mobility, noted,

> As with every data collection system, the security of information is an essential element to the solution. With increasing adoption of RFID, it is important for companies producing, implementing and using RFID to understand potential risks and rewards offered by the technology.[8]

Shields designed to hold the card when not in use vary greatly in their ability to prevent unauthorized access to the information on the tag.[9] As the use of RFID tags in credit cards and access cards becomes more widespread, systems that provide increased security will be required in order to protect consumers. Guidelines and standards, such as *NIST Special Publication 800-98: Guidelines for Securing Radio Frequency Identification (RFID) Systems* and ISO/IEC 24791 Part 6 Security, address RFID security issues. The NIST standard focuses mainly on RFID signal and database security rather than tag security.

There are some interesting developments in improving RFID tag security for retail applications:

> [MIKOH Corp.] offers a solution with its Smart&Secure™ Variable Distance technology. Unlike other RFID tags designed for use in retail applications, Smart&Secure Variable Distance allows consumers to reduce the RFID read distance simply by unfolding the top layer of the tag, which decouples the tag's antenna from its RFID chip and thereby ensures consumer privacy. If the product is returned, the tag's read distance can easily be restored by folding the tag closed again, making it fully usable in an inventory management system or reverse supply chain. The technology backing

MIKOH's Smart&Secure Variable Distance tag eliminates the threat of privacy infringements.[10]

While it is possible to extract information that thieves can use to access a cardholder's account from an RFID-enabled card, it is just as easy to do the same from the traditional magnetic stripe–equipped card, which still dominates in the United States. Because the EMV technology has proven to make RFID-encoded information more secure, the European Central Bank has recommended that banks adopt this technology and stop issuing magnetic stripe cards after 2012. The Smart Card Alliance, while noting the cost and difficulty of switching from magnetic stripe to RFID in the United States, suggests that decreases in the true cost of fraud would justify the switch.

So we would have to label this myth as plausible. Security must be taken into account, particularly for certain uses of RFID, but technological solutions to the security problems are becoming more widely available. The personal privacy issue raised by the possibility of tracking someone using RFID technology is not so much a technological issue as a cultural one. A similar question has been raised about the ability to track someone using cell phone technology. How much risk of this reduction in privacy is the public willing to accept in order to derive the benefits of RFID technology? What types of mandated safeguards would the public consider to be acceptable? These are questions still under debate and have yet to be fully resolved. Many potential applications of RFID technology revolve around the answers to these questions.

Myth 2: Tag Cost Is the Only Cost Driver for Feasibility

Tag cost is an important variable in determining the feasibility of RFID for particular applications, but it is by no means the only cost driver. An RFID tag costs more than a bar code label, so if bar code technology is sufficient for your application, then stick with it. You should not replace bar codes with more expensive RFID simply to keep up with the latest technology. In order to be successful, RFID must provide an advantage over whatever system you are currently using.

If the application you are considering involves high-value assets, such as shipping containers, semi trailers, railcars, and portable medical equipment, or if the tag is reused multiple times, such as with pallets, work-in-progress inventory (WIP) totes, and key access systems, the cost of the tag is relatively insignificant. Typically, the advantages of these types of uses greatly outweigh the cost of even the most expensive tags. A $10 WIP tote tag that is read thousands of times over its useful life results in an insignificant cost per read.

So we would label this myth as busted. RFID tag costs are a driver for feasibility, but these costs are decreasing and RFID can be a cost-effective solution for many applications.

Myth 3: Overall Costs for RFID Are High

Deployment costs as well as equipment and tag costs can be significant drivers of RFID cost feasibility. Even though RFID is a non-line-of-sight technology, there can be many issues relating to readability that must be addressed when equipping a facility for RFID. Deployment of a controlled entry system can be a relatively low-cost application. Asset tracking using HF or UHF tags and handheld readers can also be a low-cost application. For example, an HF or UHF RFID system to facilitate inventorying 1,000 physical assets with a handheld reader might cost around $1,500 to $2,000. Such a system would allow inventorying all the equipment in a room in a matter of minutes without having to move equipment and search for asset tags.

However deployment of a system to automatically track assets throughout a facility requires many carefully placed readers at multiple points in the facility. Reader placement is often not an exact science. Many things can affect the readability of a tag and these must be assessed and properly addressed. These types of installations can be quite expensive, but still provide a feasible ROI.

Success Story: RFID in Action

Campbell Hausfeld, a leading manufacturer of home improvement and automotive tools, improved distribution speed and accuracy using Zebra's RFID printers and supplies. The company had difficulty tracking production of finished goods, and tracking the shipment of those products from its distribution facilities—resulting in inventory inaccuracy and discrepancies between production and distribution. This inefficient process forced employees to manually scan each pallet that came off the line for accurate reporting of production rates.

Once deployed, the RFID system benefited Campbell with significant time savings. All products receive an RFID label created from a Zebra printer. When workers place products on a conveyer, an RFID reader tracks each item. In 10 seconds, employees can perform the same task that previously took up to 4 minutes. In addition, operations can print long plays (LPs) in bulk, instead of printing the same label 15 or 20 times, thus saving more time. In addition to numerous operational benefits, Campbell realized significant labor cost savings, as well as an 80% decrease in error rates.[11]

Chapter 6 contains four case studies taken from a variety of industries that demonstrate cost-effective implementation of RFID. These case studies provide examples of how the return on investment in RFID technology often goes beyond cost reductions due to improved equipment utilization and staff efficiency. The improvements obtained also can include improved effectiveness, organizational agility, and fewer errors by providing information that is not available in as timely a fashion with other technologies. The improvements obtained can also contribute to increased competitiveness leading to increased revenue.

So we would label this myth as busted. RFID costs have decreased dramatically and are likely to continue to decline in the future making it easier to justify the consideration of RFID technology by more organizations.

Myth 4: RFID Is the New Paradigm That Will Render Bar Codes Obsolete[12]

As indicated in the introduction to this chapter, there are applications where bar codes are sufficient and perhaps more cost effective than RFID. Sometimes RFID and bar codes are used in tandem, as shown in Case Study 6.3 in chapter 6. In this case study, CHEP uses RFID as the primary technology for managing its reusable container inventory but also uses bar code labels on the containers to enable operators to visually differentiate RFID-tagged containers from those not tagged.

Tandem use of RFID and bar code technologies is facilitated by the use of printers, such as those manufactured by Zebra, which print labels containing RFID tags, bar codes, and text. Due to its ability to read multiple, reprogrammable tags simultaneously without requiring line of sight, RFID has a number of significant performance advantages over bar coding that will see RFID taking more of the AIDC market from bar codes over time. While bar code technology currently has a larger market share, RFID is the fastest-growing segment of the automatic data capture market with forecast growth of 19.5% over the next 5 years.[13]

Ray Cronin, vice president and general manager of RFID at Intermec Technologies Corporation, recently addressed this myth. He does not foresee RFID as the death of bar codes. With the new advanced 2-D bar code technologies, more data can be encoded in the label. He sees bar codes and RFID coexisting for the foreseeable future.[14] With continued technological advances, such as 2-D bar codes, and new applications, such as the smartphone reader apps for use with embedded bar codes in advertisements, bar codes are unlikely to fade away anytime soon.

So we would label this myth as busted. Bar codes will likely be a companion technology to RFID for many years.

Myth 5: RFID Is Less Accurate and Less Dependable Than Bar Codes[15]

While read reliability for RFID in its early days was sometimes a problem under certain circumstances, the technology has advanced greatly. Cronin illustrated one aspect that renders this myth busted. When presented with a pallet of mixed goods, taking inventory using bar codes often involves depalletizing, orienting, and sequentially reading the items. Operator inattention and boredom can lead to missed reads. With RFID the entire contents of the pallet can be read simultaneously without depalletizing and repositioning of the boxes.

So we would consider this myth busted. In some cases accuracy and dependability with RFID can exceed those of bar codes.

Summary

So all the myths discussed in this chapter have some basis in fact. Some are remnants from the early days of RFID, while others are from issues still being addressed and await full resolution. The lesson to take from this discussion is to carefully research your intended application for RFID. Be sure that RFID is the best technological application for your intended use. Be aware of the limitations as well as the capabilities of RFID. Consider all the costs and benefits—not just the obvious ones—when justifying your RFID application.

CHAPTER 5

Implementing RFID

Implementation of RFID is a significant investment for any organization of any size. Some companies implementing the technology may be doing so only to comply with a mandate from their supply chain customers. These companies are being reactive in their focus by implementing a simple slap-and-ship system that fulfills the short-term requirement. They are missing the opportunity to take advantage of the capabilities of RFID to improve their internal operations. Companies that take a more proactive approach to system design and implementation focus on the benefits that RFID can provide for their company. The following are some examples of the benefits that can provide a return on investment for companies that take a proactive approach and implement the system properly:[1]

- Reduced stock outs
- Enhanced security and reduced shrinkage
- Improved delivery receipt and reconciliation processes
- Improved management of time-sensitive goods
- Better inventory and warehouse management
- Better defect tracking and recall management
- Better product velocity

Implementation is generally where initiatives of any type will fail if they are destined to do so. Walmart's initial implementation effort of pushing RFID down their supply chain at the case and pallet level was not as successful as they wanted. However, the retailer is now taking a much different approach to implementing RFID by focusing on the item level. They are first deploying the technology with their suppliers for men's jeans and basics so they can track their inventory at the item level. Walmart's plan is to then expand the use of the technology by working with other suppliers while trying to be sensitive to the impact of the cost on the suppliers. Their effort is designed to help Walmart suppliers move beyond the idea that using RFID is simply a cost of doing business with them and enable them to reap real benefits from the information the technology can provide, such as customers' preferred style and purchasing patterns.

An off-the-shelf solution for an RFID implementation is not always a practical option for a company with a challenging work environment. Obstacles in the environment include fluids, metals, and equipment that may emit RF signals that could interfere with RFID communication. Ordinary items that are taken for granted in any other environment, such as a cordless phone, could interfere with an RFID system. The types of products that are being tagged may present problems if they contain metal or liquids. In these cases, the physical environment presents obstacles that must be addressed during implementation.

Prior to implementing an RFID system, an organization has to decide what information is important for them to gather as well as how that information will be integrated into the organization's enterprise resource planning (ERP) system if one is utilized. There are several considerations pertaining to the system's scalability and flexibility:[2]

- Can the ERP system infrastructure support the massive amounts of data resulting from the RFID system?
- What is the scalability of the system?
- Can the ERP system provide a business context for the RFID data to identify problems and opportunities?
- What technologies enhance existing business processes?

Managing the RFID Implementation Project

Managing an RFID implementation will take planning and testing before acquisition and deployment of the physical system begins. The following are some of the things that will need to be done in advance of a successful RFID deployment:

- Identify the purpose for using RFID
- Select the appropriate type of RFID
- Identify the best system fit

- Identify the best level to tag
- Identify the best RFID tag to use
- Prepare the project plan
- Plan the training program
- Monitor the system

Identify the Purpose for Using RFID

The first question an organization should examine relates to whether or not RFID is the right technology for the job. Clearly stating the purpose of using RFID is essential. While RFID is an extraordinary technology, it could be that another technology, such as bar coding, would be just as useful and less costly. By clearly identifying the intended purpose, the organization can decide the best approach. There are some questions to ask when identifying the purpose for using RFID:

- What are the benefits your organization is seeking from the technology?
- What information will be useful for your organization?
- How frequently does that information need to be updated?
- Who will be responsible for the information?
- Who will be responsible for the system?
- Is RFID the best technology for this purpose?
- What is the expected return versus the expected investment?

Identifying the purpose is like writing the objectives for a scope of work for a strategic project. The focus is on defining how the organization is going to better meet its or its customers' needs through this implementation. Once the purpose of the implementation project is identified, the next step is identifying the appropriate type of RFID to use.

Select the Appropriate Type of RFID

The next decision that needs to be made is whether active or passive RFID best matches the purpose of the project and the needs of the organization. The implementation team must continually refer back to the purpose of the system. The choice may well end up being passive technology because of cost issues. If that is the case, then the implementation team will need to choose between low frequency, high frequency, and ultra high frequency systems. To assist in these choices the situation can be analyzed by asking some questions:

- What is the maximum read distance for the intended application?
- Will the system have to work inside and outside?
- How long of a time period will the item need to be monitored?
- How much need for privacy and security is there?
- How much information needs to be included on the tag?

Once the type of RFID is decided, then the implementation team should begin to evaluate the best system fit.

Identify the Best System Fit

Another decision is the selection of the appropriate system to fit the situation of the organization. The initial work that will need to be completed at this stage is a scan of the environment that the system will need to operate in. Is the environment going to be dense with tags? If so we need to select a system that will operate best in that environment. Does the reader need to be user friendly? Again we would need to select a system that is easier to use. Another question might go back to the purpose of the system, and that is, are we simply tracking inventory or are we trying to match inventory to someone or something? This question can help to determine if a fixed position reader is needed or if a handheld unit will work.

The need for middleware to get the data collected into a usable form in a database will be determined by the type of RFID system selected. As previously stated, most RFID readers have a software development kit (SDK) package included so some programming may be necessary.

Antenna polarization and setup also play a vital role at this decision point. For example, are you in a manufacturing environment where the tags would only be read at a certain position? If so a linearly polarized antenna might provide the best coverage in this circumstance. However, if the reads have to take place once the items are palletized then a circularly polarized antenna might provide the best coverage. In addition to antenna polarization, antenna placement needs to be a concern. The team would need to determine if there is a portal through which tagged items move to be read that needs to be monitored or if there needs to be more of a chandelier approach (Figure 5.1), which provides total read coverage for a building or an area within a building.

A site analysis is also appropriate at this time. The team would want to analyze the situation to determine if there are corners that might create dead space where a signal could not be read. They would need to look at equipment in the space to determine if it would create noise (other signals) that might interfere with the RF signal. As discussed earlier, a simple cordless phone could disrupt the ability of the technology to obtain a read. The implementation team might use an RF spectrum analyzer to analyze spurious signals in the area and to determine where signal strength might be best.

Identify the Best Level to Tag

An analysis of the level of tagging is also necessary at this point. As discussed earlier, most organizations are currently tagging at the pallet and case level. However, depending on the cost of the item, some organizations are choosing

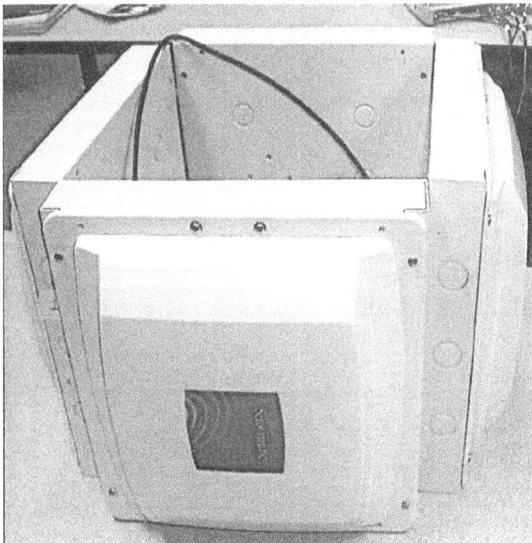

Figure 5.1. Four-antenna RFID reader chandelier array for area monitoring.

Photograph courtesy of the Sower Business Technology Laboratory, College of Business Administration, Sam Houston State University.

to now tag at the item level. The implementation team should return to the initial questions: What is the purpose of the system and what type of information do we need? Once the level of tagging has been established, then the implementation team's attention must turn to selecting the best tag to use.

Identify the Best RFID Tag to Use

As described earlier in the book, tags vary in sensitivity, size, and shape. The implementation team will need to look at the results of the analyses to this point and determine the read range capability needed. Once the read range necessary is established, then the implementation team must test a variety of tags to identify the one that will be most useful in collecting the desired data (Table 5.1).

The implementation team will also need to consider the harshness of the environment during tag selection. Are there extreme temperature conditions in the environment? Is the environment damp? Is there a lot of metal in the environment? What is the product that is being tagged? Is there metal or liquid in the product itself? How will the product be handled and what type of equipment will be used during movement of the product? All these questions should help the team analyze the situation and decide the type of tag needed. The following case study provides an overview of the conduct of an RFID implementation project.

Table 5.1. Examples of Tag Read Ranges

Part #s: Avery Dennison inlays	Optimal read range specified (ft.)	Maximum read range obtained (ft.)
AD-814 600196	<5	10
AD-833 600184	<2	39
AD-828 600208	<5	30
AD-223 600193	<20	57
AD-805 600186	<10	15
AD-824 600188	<15	35
AD-827 600211	10–20	45
AD-240 600218	<30	45
AD-815 600220	3–5	38

Results from tests conducted by Dr. Jeremy Bellah and student Cerise Ashmore in the SHSU Sower Business Technology Laboratory using an Impinj Speedway Reader.

RFID and Asset Tracking Experience

*By Pearl M. Wright, President, 4W Solutions, and
L. Tony Wright, Vice President, 4W Solutions**

4W Solutions (4W) is a small, woman-owned business providing professional services to public and private organizations. 4W is focused on providing outsourcing of extraordinary professionals who can "do whatever it takes" to solve our customer needs. Today 4W provides federal and commercial clients with a full spectrum of professional, technical, and administrative services including: Asset and Inventory Management and Logistics Services utilizing RFID, Procurement and Contract Administration; Project Management, and other Information Technology (IT) support services.

When 4W expanded into the RFID market several years ago, we attended many RFID webinars, took RFID training offered by Alien Technologies, and immediately started marketing our RFID expertise into the NASA community where we already had a good reputation for delivering quality products and services. We realized that in order to be a player in this market, we needed past performance and unfortunately did not possess it at that time. The training and credentials we received were not enough. We needed to demonstrate our understanding of RFID and have a customer and success story.

We soon found a small business in California named Mannequin Madness who had recently won a grant from Intel Corporation to implement RFID to track its mannequin inventory. We were successful in writing a winning proposal that this customer accepted that allowed us to implement RFID for them. Customers would come to Mannequin Madness and give them a wish list such as "I am looking for a headless mannequin in the seated position" and as a result the customer needed a way to quickly locate each piece and identify the items characteristics (i.e., full mannequin, torso, head, headless, seated, standing, fabric, fiberglass, etc.) in one central database. In addition, the customer wanted to use RFID to integrate different

---

* Used with permission.

business software platforms to help better manage sales and inventory systems. While this all was a daunting task, the customer was still excited but frustrated by not being able to find a vendor that could service a business as small as hers.

Due to the breadth of the scope of services, we quickly realized that this was not the typical RFID project; however, it would give us the ability to demonstrate our competencies in project management, business process and workflow analysis; RFID and Barcode Integration and Application Development, physical Site Assessment; Equipment selection, Utilization and Optimization; Rapid Prototyping; and Systems Validation and Verification.

To start, we set out to get an understanding of the daily operations of the business, how the RFID system would operate and any special needs. This required an in depth analysis of the customer's existing inventory procedures, accounting procedures, and eCommerce software. Next we needed to know the number of users and locations the RFID system would be utilized for and soon discovered that there would be up to three locations where the system would be used and the inventory at those locations would all have to be seamlessly integrated in to the database.

As part of our agreement and scope of work, 4W designed a seamless integration of RFID into existing operations with an improved return on investment in terms of labor efficiency, inventory control, sales, reporting, and business expansion. We determined that RFID should be integrated at the receiving, storage, and shipping points; all interface points for the technology that required RFID tagging, scanning, and database input. **Receiving**—when new inventory arrives; the mannequins would be tagged for tracking. In addition, the receiving staff would input information that would be programmed onto the RFID tag. **Storage**—once the inventory reached the storage facility, it would have been tagged and therefore managed utilizing a handheld reader. Inventory management would include placement, relocation, audits, and removal from inventory. **Shipping**—when a mannequin was sold or leased, it would be scanned again for real time inventory tracking and that information would be transmitted back to the customer centralized database.

Upon completion of this analysis, we then made a site visit to assess the physical layout of the space and identify any potential items that could interfere with the read range of tags and readers such as fluorescent lighting, metal shelving, or any other areas that may require immediate attention and/or removal to achieve the desired read range. We performed some preliminary testing utilizing the Symbol 9000 RFID reader demo program and were able to determine various read distances and identify some interference, which only occurred when a tag was placed directly onto a metal part.

Taking all the aforementioned information from the site visit we conducted regular meetings with the customer to work on customization of the software itself. For example, we wanted to be clear on the type of data that must be captured by the RFID system such as names and values of the inventory. In addition, we had to determine what fields we could manipulate in the customer's existing eCommerce software system that would allow us to integrate the data read from the tags.

We then proceeded with the hardware selection and testing, which mostly consisted of identifying the type of tag and reader we would use as well as how the tags would be attached to the mannequins. We initially looked at utilizing passive tags from Alien Technologies but the read range was the desired 20 ft. that we had previously tested. As a result, we located a manufacturer located in Canada that had some passive tags that would give us the desired read range and we could also design the tag itself to make the attachment and removal easier for the customer. We decided on a dog tag shaped tag with four holes in each corner to allow for the insertion of an elastic cord so the tag could be attached to a mannequin's arm, leg, torso, or neck. Lastly, due to the multiple locations and the warehouse environment it was determined to be in the best interest of the customer to utilize the Symbol 9000 handheld RFID reader, which was ruggedized for use in warehouses and other unique facilities.

Our team of developers analyzed the results of the workflow analysis, hardware selection and testing as other special requirements of the customer and developed the handheld application. This consisted of developing a data dictionary for all the mannequin parts and characteristics (i.e., boy/girl, arm, leg, head, torso, standing, seated, manufacturer, condition of the mannequin, as well as the lease and sales price). The developers then proceeded to design the interface between the customer's existing inventory management system and the RFID application. This was critical as it also would play a larger role in determining the handheld screens that the user would ultimately see when using the handheld. We also had to determine the backup procedures to maintain data integrity at all times and write training documents for all end users.

Upon completion of the software programming and testing, we then scheduled a delivery visit to perform integration testing and train Mannequin Madness personnel. Once the testing was determined to be successful and accepted by the customer, we proceeded to the "Go Live" stage where we created the inventory baseline; which required our team to go to each of the customer's sites and tag the existing inventory, scan the existing inventory and populate the customer's existing inventory control module with data. We then verified the data integrity and the interface between RFID software, the customer's eCommerce and overall inventory control.

We then provided the customer with a detailed training manual that was written by the 4W team of developers and trained all the customer's employees on how to use the system and what to expect when the system is used properly.

4W Solutions turnkey project in RFID-based inventory management required an innovative solution under demanding system and operational constraints. In an atypical network-disconnected RFID environment, we designed and built an RFID warehousing system for a small business with various product materials in various physical environments. The RFID application needed to interface with a web-based backend that was under development by another company. 4W took the lead in analyzing the business processes and workflows, capturing the system requirements, defining intervendor data interfaces, and coordinating the system documentation.

4W played an integral role in the design and technical leadership of this RFID project. The resulting system met the customers' needs and is scalable to coincide with business growth.

Setting RFID in Motion

Prepare the Project Plan

Once the implementation team has completed its analysis of the situation, then a plan must be developed to set the RFID system implementation in motion. As previously stated, there are no guaranteed turnkey systems for every type of RFID implementation. As with any technology implementation, there will be some variation in how the system is set up and interacts in its environment. However, with proper analysis of the situation, the information gathered should provide enough detail to create a proper implementation plan. The scope of the project should already be in place as a result of the analysis. The next step in the plan will be scheduling the installation process. The scan of the physical environment should provide enough information to identify the details of the process. The details can be analyzed to determine the time necessary for installation.

At this stage there is sufficient information to project a return on investment (ROI). It is important when calculating the ROI to include the financial impact of all aspects of the implementation. RFID is much broader in reach and impact than simply a network or information technology investment.

> You must understand your supply chain and the transformative impact of RFID technology before trying to quantify a project. RFID is not a magic bullet but when leveraged properly it will bring value to most supply chains. And diligence does pay off for those companies that take the time and consider the process, technical and financial components of an ROI analysis.[3]

For example, a company determined that having a sales associate off the sales floor (e.g., conducting an inventory) during an off-peak sales period resulted in an average of $20 in lost sales per store. They calculated that the annual sales increase for all 2,000 stores would be $200,000 per year per sales associate hour gained. So for every hour that RFID decreases store inventory time in each of its stores, the company would gain $200,000 in sales per year.[4] In addition to the increased sales, the company should see an increase in customer satisfaction, which should also have monetary value.

Plan the Training Program

As the system is being developed, the implementation team needs to create training manuals and plans for training employees. As part of the implementation process, it is necessary to train employees about how the system will work. Just as important as knowing how the system works, the employees need to know how to use the information generated by the system. The success or failure of the system will depend on the immediate and continued training of employees who are using the technology or are using the information generated by the technology.

Monitor the System

Once the system is in place and the employees are trained in the use of RFID technology, then a system for monitoring and control must be implemented as well. It is necessary to determine that all parts of the system are operating as intended. There are some tools that might be good to have for monitoring the system. For example, Venture Research, Inc. has a tool for determining whether an antenna is operating (Figure 5.2). The readers should be periodically tested to ensure that they are operating properly. In addition, as with any environment, the surroundings are changing. Other materials are brought in and the systems must be monitored to determine if these materials interrupt the ability of the RFID system to perform. In addition to monitoring the technical aspects of the system, it is important at this stage to verify that the RFID system is meeting its purposes and is achieving its projected ROI.

Summary

This chapter outlined a basic process for planning and executing an RFID implementation. Details of implementations vary widely depending on the specific application; however, all should include the components discussed. Experienced hardware providers and systems integrators have

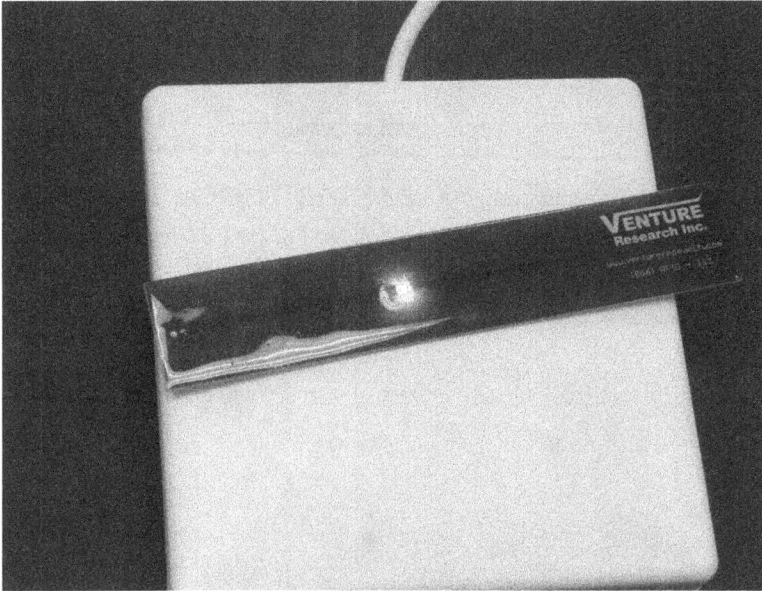

Figure 5.2. Radio frequency signal tool for verifying antenna operation.

Photograph courtesy of the Sower Business Technology Laboratory, College of Business Administration, Sam Houston State University.

experience in a wide variety of RFID implementations and can provide valuable expertise that will reduce risk. The following are best practices for RFID implementations:[5]

1. Passive RFID is generally a good choice for companies seeking benefits of an automated inventory control system.
2. Make sure your company is purchasing the hardware that achieves the required read rates.
3. Choose the equipment that fits your purpose.
4. Choosing one tag that works for all your assets can prevent confusion and reduce the cost of deployment.
5. Innovative tagging can help tag even the smallest assets.
6. Creating a clear and simple procedure for tag placement can prevent later problems.
7. Do application testing in the actual environment to uncover any hidden issues.

8. Other equipment can interfere with the deployment; test and analyze the area while work is going on.

9. Experimentation is important because RFID can be a solution for applications previously deemed impossible.

Chapter 7 discusses the future for RFID. Obviously, the more novel the RFID use, the greater the unknowns. For creative innovations, it is even more important to follow a logical implementation process and to locate experienced equipment providers in order to reduce overall project risk.

CHAPTER 6

Business Cases for RFID

This chapter contains a diverse selection of actual case studies illustrating the use of RFID in a wide variety of industries to show the diversity of current uses of RFID technology. These case studies are a sampling rather than an exhaustive list of the many applications and industries in which RFID is currently in use. The case studies were selected to demonstrate both traditional and innovative uses of RFID and to stimulate thought about how you might improve your operations through the use of RFID.

Case Study 6.1 discusses how Bon Secours Richmond Health System uses RFID to track key equipment, such as IV pumps and wheelchairs, within its hospitals. Before RFID was implemented, it was often difficult to locate key equipment when needed. This resulted in low equipment utilization, purchase of unneeded equipment, and process delays. After implementation, equipment utilization jumped from 40% to 90%. The hospital estimates it saves $2 million annually in equipment rental, losses, and service costs. Staff overtime hours have also been reduced. Along with the cost reductions, revenue has also increased because the increased productivity allows more surgical procedures to be accomplished without facility expansion.

Case Study 6.2 discusses how Throttleman, a European clothing retailer, uses RFID to reduce the lead time to receive clothing into its distribution facilities. With a read accuracy of 99.9%, the RFID system is quicker and more accurate than previous systems. The RFID system increases the visibility of inventory and facilitates cross-docking, which has reduced Throttleman's need for warehouse space by 60%. In implementing the RFID system, Throttleman is able to increase retail sales by restocking their shelves faster and more accurately.

Case Study 6.3 discusses how CHEP, a pallet and container pooling services company operating in Europe, uses RFID to track 150,000 foldable large containers throughout Europe. The result has been improved accountability of containers worth about €150 ($188) apiece, improved tracking, and improved inspection data. In addition, the system has increased brand recognition for CHEP throughout Europe.

Case Study 6.4 discusses how the Santa Clara County Crime Laboratory tracks movement of all evidence throughout its entire evaluation cycle using RFID. The advantage of RFID over bar codes is that the laboratory knows where any one particular piece of evidence is at any one time and whom it has been assigned to. The RFID system provides a quantifiable increase in process turnaround time, which is important to the laboratory since it receives more than 35,000 pieces of evidence per year. In addition, the system provides database access to multiple law enforcement agencies, allowing the linking of evidence from crimes across different jurisdictions.

CASE STUDY 6.1

Using RFID to Track Equipment and Patients*

Company: Bon Secours Richmond Health System
http://www.bonsecours.com
Application: Tracking key hospital equipment
Area of Use: Hospital
Challenge: Inability to locate key equipment quickly, resulting in equipment utilization of 40%
Solution:
- 11,000 assets were equipped with RFID tags.
- Patients are provided with RFID tag–equipped ID bracelets.
- RFID system integrated in with the hospital's computer system.

Benefits:
- Realized $2 million annual savings on equipment rental, losses, and service costs
- Increased equipment utilization to 90%
- Reduced operating room turnover time
- Increased productivity and reduced overtime

After implementing radio frequency identification technology, a health system has saved $2 million a year, improved efficiency, decreased labor costs, and increased operating room capacity.

Summary

In 2004, Bon Secours Richmond Health System, Richmond, Va., began using radio frequency identification (RFID) technology to track equipment.

---

* Used with permission from Healthcare Cost Containment, February 2011. Copyright © Healthcare Financial Management Association, http://www.hfma.org.

The technology employs radio frequency signals to remotely locate equipment that has been marked with bar codes.

Since installing the technology, Bon Secours Richmond, a system of four hospitals and 875 beds, has saved almost $2 million annually. The technology has been so effective that the health system has implemented additional RFID initiatives, including tracking patients in the operating room (OR), which has resulted in improved efficiencies and greater volume.

Improved Utilization

Bon Secours worked with a locally based technology company to become a beta site for RFID technology, which was deployed on 11,000 assets, such as IV pumps, wheelchairs, stretchers, and beds. Each item was given a bar code embedded with an RFID tag, or microchip.

The microchip transmits identification data to an RFID reader, which in turn sends those data to the hospital's computer system, enabling the supply to be tracked.

Prior to implementation of this technology, Bon Secours faced problems typical to large health systems. Equipment was often sitting unused in a hallway on one patient care floor, while staff on another floor were in need of the equipment but unable to easily locate it. With IV pumps, for instance, the health system had a utilization rate of only 40 percent, says Kathy Santini, RN, vice president of surgical services. "The problem was nobody knew where all those pumps were. Now, our utilization of those pumps is 90 percent," she says.

The savings resulted from reducing the quantity of rental equipment used in the four hospitals by 38 percent and decreasing the incidence of lost and stolen equipment by 50 percent. Equipment service costs were also reduced by 15 percent.

The tracking system has also helped with infection control by ensuring that equipment receives preventive maintenance at the appropriate time. For example, once a patient care bed is disconnected from all monitoring devices, the technology transmits that information to the computer system. So, rather than having a bed sitting in a hallway until someone realizes it's ready for maintenance, immediate notification is sent to housekeeping, reducing the likelihood that the bed will be reused before being properly cleaned.

Efficiencies in the OR

Almost two years ago, Bon Secours took the technology a step further—using RFID in combination with a Six Sigma process improvement technique to reduce OR turnover time by 50 percent in surgical services at its largest hospital, St. Mary's Hospital, which has 20 inpatient operating rooms.

Upon arrival to the admitting room, patients are given a regular identification bracelet and one implanted with an RFID chip. "So, we can tell immediately when those patients are in the system," Santini says. Although the Six Sigma technique supplied specific targets and methods for improvement, the RFID technology allowed patients to be tracked at the various steps in the surgical process.

Each clinician in the pre- and postoperative process completes his or her work and then lets everyone else know, by scanning the RFID bracelet, that the patient is ready for the next step in the process. For example, a holding room nurse performs a readiness assessment, then creates a note on the computer system indicating that the holding room has cleared the patient, letting the anesthesiologist know that the patient is ready for him. When the surgery is complete, the patient's RFID bracelet sends a signal to the computer that the patient is leaving the OR, alerting a clinical team that the room is ready to be cleaned and prepped for the next patient.

An additional benefit of the RFID system is that any instrument or piece of equipment that is included on the surgeon's preference list, but not available on or near the surgical case cart, can be located quickly via the RFID system.

Before implementing the RFID technology and the Six Sigma system, OR turnover time at St. Mary's averaged about 45 minutes; the goal was to reduce turnover time to 20 minutes, a target the staff was reaching just 10 percent of the time, Santini says.

Because the caseload in the inpatient OR rooms includes major surgeries, such as total joint replacements, craniotomies, and open heart, Santini says setting a 20-minute turnover time in between patients represents an aggressive target.

One year after implementation, staff were able to reach the target turnover time about 85 percent of the time—good, but not good enough. "Bon Secours is a type-A organization, and we always believe that our performance should be in the top decile. So we strive to reach our target 90 percent of the time or more," she says.

Part of the improvement in turnover time has resulted from increased efficiency. Santini says the number of phone calls made among departments in the OR is down 75 percent because everyone has access to patient status information on the computer. Santini says processes are continuing to be refined to reach the organization's target turnover rate.

Benefits in OR and Beyond

Use of RFID in the OR has helped improve productivity, decrease costs, and enhance the opportunity for increasing revenue. Because ORs are being prepped faster, surgeons can use the additional time to add a case to their block of time in the OR schedule. Santini says as the hospital's surgical caseload has increased, so has revenue. "We figured out we could add about $5 million, minimum, to our bottom line with additional cases," she says. In addition, productivity is in excess of 100 percent, overtime is less than 2 percent of labor costs, which Santini says is typically 3 percent for most hospitals, and total cost per patient has decreased annually.

Bon Secours has since rolled out the new OR turnover process at St. Francis Hospital, which has the system's second busiest OR, and will eventually use it at the organization's other two hospitals. In the meantime, plans call for implementing the system in the emergency department at both St. Mary's and St. Francis.

The health system also plans to use the RFID system to monitor hospital-acquired infections. One initiative will track whether patient care staff are washing their hands in patient rooms.

Soap dispensers will be wired to send signals to a computer when the dispensers have been used. The technology also will be used to alert housekeeping when a room is ready for cleaning and alert clinical staff when the room is available for a patient.

Additionally, the technology will be used to help monitor patients with Alzheimer's disease by using signals to notify hospital staff when a patient has left either the room or the floor. "There are all kinds of things you can do with RFID technology," Santini says.

CASE STUDY 6.2

*European Retailer Throttleman Improves Supply Chain With RFID**

Company: Throttleman, http://www.throttleman.com

Application: Item-level tracking for fashion retailer

Area of Use: Distribution center

Tag Supplier: Alien Technology

Tags: 866 MHz

Systems Integrator: Creativesystems, http://www.creativesystems.pt

Challenge: Improve retail supply chain to stock stores more quickly

Solution: RFID hang tags, middleware, and reader

Toolset:

- EPC-compliant Alien Technology Corporation Gen 2 Squiggle inlay Converted
- Sybase RFID Anywhere middleware

Benefits:

- Tag 1.5 million garments through the supply chain, most of which come from Asia to Europe
- Reduced the time clothing spends in the distribution center from 5 days to 24 hours
- Restock retail shelves more quickly and accurately creates greater opportunity for sales
- Saved 60% on space in distribution center

Throttleman is a European fashion retailer with attitude. Throttleman-branded clothing for men, kids, and women is known for original, fresh design, but what's stylish now can quickly fade from view.

Challenge

To stay ahead of trends, Throttleman needs to get its distinctive, original styles to its stores quickly and keep the shelves stocked with the hottest items. To meet these objectives, Throttleman needed to reduce the lead time for receiving clothing into its distribution centers. As the company was adding new lines of clothing, stock in the distribution centers was growing, and space was growing scarce.

Additionally, Throttleman didn't always have an instant picture of the items actually in its distribution center compared to what the ERP system showed was in stock. To meet these challenges, Throttleman integrated RFID into its global supply chain.

Solution

Throttleman worked with Iberian systems integrator Creativesystems to create an RFID solution that would improve the speed and efficiency of its supply chain from Asia to Europe.

UHF RFID is gaining momentum over HF RFID for item-level tracking. UHF Gen 2 RFID has hit the sweet spot of price/performance, and the price of a Gen 2 passive tag is measured in cents. Plus, industry standards like Gen 2 RFID deliver a high level of interoperability, which has created a broad ecosystem of vendors. Alien Technology Squiggle is an EPC-compliant tag designed for global operation in the 860 MHz to 960 MHz frequency spectrum, so the tags can be used successfully across the unique operating frequencies used in the Americas, Europe, Asia and Africa. The Squiggle is ideal for apparel and airline baggage.

Results

Throttleman has reduced the lead time to receive apparel into its distribution centers and has achieved its goals for on-time shipments to retail stores. It has eliminated problems with space constraints in the warehouse and gained end-to-end visibility into the supply chain.

"The underlying purpose of tagging 1.5 million garments, each with a UHF RFID tag, was to enhance the throughput of garments through the distribution centers," says Miguel Maya, associate general director for Throttleman. "By reducing the time required to restock retail shelves, Throttleman will realize greater revenues. To accomplish this, we needed the fastest and most dependable UHF Gen 2 tag in the marketplace today."

Clothing used to spend up to five days in the supply chain. Now apparel spends less than 24 hours. With Throttleman's fresh designs and its stylish customers, getting clothing on the retail shelves faster can increase same-store sales. Plus, the most desirable clothing can be sold at full price longer and not have to be discounted once it becomes less in demand.

"Throttleman can drive more sales by restocking their shelves faster and more accurately," says Francisco Teixeira e Melo, managing director at Creativesystems.

Clothing is tagged at the manufacturers in India, with conversion and encoding done locally, and then the garments are boxed and shipped to Throttleman's distribution centers in Portugal. When the boxes are received, they are scanned by the RFID reader tunnel and the contents of each box are read in seconds. The RFID tunnel ensures a consistent flow of boxes, and it also shields the reader from external interference, which reduces unwanted readings.

The system can read 15,000 garments per hour with an accuracy of 99.9 percent. Teixeira e Melo says there can be issues with the shadowing of tags, particularly if the garment fabric is very thin or silky. However, the manufacturer is incented to fix any problems with the accuracy of the tags, because Throttleman only pays for garments that are validated by the RFID system. As the garment tags are read, the system automatically compares the list of scanned items to the packing slip. Any discrepancies trigger an alert to check the contents of the box.

"The RFID system is quicker and it reduces error," says Teixeira e Melo. "Normally, if you receive 100 items of the same product, you read one and count it as 100. With the new system, Throttleman checks every item in every size and if there's one item that's misplaced, they can spot it right away."

Once the garments are validated, they are cross-docked for delivery to one of Throttleman's 60 retail locations. The garments are labeled with the name of the destination store and go into expediting for shipment. Throttleman no longer needs to warehouse items, as garments are ready to be shipped once they are validated.

"Throttleman saves an average of 60 percent in warehouse space because of cross-docking, as compared to doing reception the standard way," says Teixeira e Melo. Static stock no longer has to be warehoused, as stock is sent directly to the stores.

The RetailID platform uses Sybase RFID Anywhere software to manage and filter the information from the RFID readers. The system is also integrated with Throttleman's ERP system, so Throttleman can also use the RetailID platform to manage, control and track its products.

Next Steps

Now that RFID has solved Throttleman's issues in the supply chain, the company is looking toward RFID applications in its retail stores. It plans to conduct real-time inventory using the RetailID platform. RetailID also allows for new channels of merchandising, such as the Magicmirror. Magicmirror is an RFID-enabled mirror and digital display that customers can use to receive automated customer service while trying on clothing.

CASE STUDY 6.3

CHEP Tracks Auto-Part Containers in Europe*

Company: CHEP, http://www.chep.com

Application: Container tracking into and out of pallet and container pool service facilities

Area of Use: CHEP European facilities

Tag Supplier: RF Identics

Tags: Impinj EPC Gen 2 chips

Systems Integrator: In-house with help from Infosys

Challenge: Track industrial-grade plastic containers to remove unnecessary cost in the supply chain

Solution:

- RF Identics RFID tags containing Impinj Gen 2 chips
- Infosys code for Microsoft's BizTalk, SAP's Auto ID Infrastructure (AII) and Event Management (EM) software
- Sirit RFID interrogators

Benefits:

- Tag 150,000 foldable large containers for use throughout Europe
- Improved accountability of containers
- Improved tracking and inspection data
- Better brand recognition for CHEP

Pallet and container pooling services company CHEP is using EPC Gen 2 tags to track the shipment, receipt, inspection, and repair of 150,000 returnable plastic containers.

---

* Original case study by Rhea Wessel. Used with permission from *RFID Journal*.

Challenge

CHEP, a pallet and container pooling services company owned by Australia-based Brambles, is running an RFID-based application that tracks returnable containers for the automotive industry at its facilities in countries across Europe, according to Floris Kleijn, CHEP's director of RFID, as a service in Europe, the Middle East and Africa (EMEA).

The industrial-grade plastic containers, known as foldable large containers (FLCs), are used to transport large automotive parts from the supplier to the assembler of a vehicle. CHEP issues, collects and conditions the containers from its service centers.

As CHEP launched the project, it decided to approach the idea of tracking containers by considering not only the benefits such an application could bring to the company, but also those that could be delivered to automotive suppliers, such as an enhanced ability to locate goods within the supply chain.

Solution

CHEP opted to implement and test the application itself before involving clients in developing and operating the RFID system. It wanted to first prove to the market that it could build a cross-border RFID application. Currently, CHEP shares information regarding the movement of containers into and out of its facilities with customers; in the future, it hopes to offer RFID-based tracking services for suppliers.

The implementation of the RFID application was managed in house by CHEP, with help from systems integrator Infosys, which wrote code for the software used in the application, based on Microsoft's BizTalk and SAP's Auto ID Infrastructure (AII) and Event Management (EM) software. CHEP put the tracking application into operation in May 2008, and now has 150,000 tagged FLCs in circulation. The tags, produced by RF Identics and containing Impinj EPC Gen 2 chips, are attached to the container's underside, with two bar-coded labels applied to the external sides to enable operators to visually differentiate tagged containers from those not tagged. RFID interrogators manufactured by Sirit are being installed at nine facilities in Germany, Hungary, the United Kingdom, Turkey, Poland, Spain and France. Each facility has an average of two dock-door portal readers, with a total of 14 handhelds employed throughout the system.

CHEP's container-tracking process includes four read points: shipment, receiving, inspection and post-repair. First, tagged containers are identified as they are moved on a forklift through the RFID portal at the dock door en route to CHEP's customers—automotive parts suppliers. The forklift driver pulls up a work order from SAP software on the touch screen of his onboard computer, then selects the dock door through which he plans to drive. The order number identifies the name of the company to which the containers are being shipped, thereby associating the customer with those particular containers. When empty containers are returned to CHEP, the same process happens in reverse.

Upon return, the containers must be inspected to determine if repairs are necessary. An operator spreads the containers out on the floor, using a handheld interrogator with a touch screen to read their tags. If he sees damage, the operator notes it to the system by selecting the type of damage from menus on the screen. Once a container has been repaired, the operator utilizes the handheld to read the tag and record the work done. Because the system knows which customer the container was shipped to, and since CHEP knows which automakers its clients supply, the company can determine the "trading channel" the container was circulating in and collect damage statistics by channel. "After analyzing variance in damage statistics, we can talk to our customers about how to avoid damage," says Kleijn, who described the system at RFID Journal LIVE! Europe, held in Prague. "This will help remove unnecessary cost from the supply chain."

Results

The project's initial goal was to prove CHEP could gain value from using RFID on returnable assets so it could have a credible conversation about extending benefits to customers. The project, Kleijn says, has indeed confirmed the application offers better accountability for containers, including those that are damaged, and provides better brand recognition for CHEP—something that helps automakers return the proper containers to the company. What's more, the system allows CHEP to easily track inspection and repair data. Before the RFID application was implemented, containers—worth about €150 ($188) apiece—were not uniquely identified.

Next Steps

The next challenge for the application, Kleijn says, involves expanding it to its customers' premises. By doing so, CHEP could provide suppliers with real-time information regarding the location of their goods in the supply chain, thereby helping those companies reduce their inventory. Such data could also be valuable if a firm needed to switch from building one model of a vehicle to another on short notice. "Right now we track the container ID when it leaves, and when it comes back to CHEP facilities," Kleijn says. "We know how long it is in the field. But if a customer associated the contents of the container with the container ID, it could use the software to know where specific parts are in the supply chain. With the system we have in place today, we can now approach the customer to work with us to build the association between the part number and the container ID."

CHEP was presented with an eLogistics Award from AKJ Automotive, an association of automotive manufacturers. The award was for the largest cross-border RFID application for automotive containers in Europe. In its press release, AKJ noted, "CHEP's RFID initiative will provide significant benefits to the automotive industry, delivering control, cost savings and improving the efficiency of the supply chain." Kleijn states, "We are very pleased that the system is working well, and is already demonstrating the positive benefits that RFID can deliver across the automotive supply chain."

CASE STUDY 6.4

Santa Clara County Crime Laboratory Solves Evidence Tracking Challenge With RFID*

Company: Santa Clara County Crime Laboratory

Application: Evidence tracking

Area of Use: 4-story, 90,000 sq. ft. laboratory facility in Santa Clara, CA

RFID Supplier: Alien Technology

Integrator: CIBER, Inc.

Status: Production

Tags: 902–928 MHz

Range: 30 ft. (Range is dependent on many factors)

Challenge:

- Allow criminalists and toxicologists to efficiently check evidence in and out of property lockers
- Laboratory analyzes 35,000+ pieces of evidence annually from multiple law enforcement agencies

Solution:

- All evidence is tagged with RFID
- RFID readers located in major passageways
- RFID tracking system links to the Laboratory Information Management System (LIMS) database
- Toolset includes:
  - Alien ALR-9650 readers
  - Disposable Squiggle tags

Benefits:

- Efficient evidence tracking in expansive, multistory crime laboratory
- Fast RFID readers allow laboratory staff to easily check-in/check-out evidence

Solving crime is no easy business. It involves disciplined law enforcement, a thorough investigation and collection of facts, and extensive evidence testing performed by well-trained teams of criminalists and toxicologists. With new advances in forensic science that include mitochondrial DNA sampling, crime laboratories have become the vital link in helping solve crimes, even decades-old cold cases. The mystery now is how should a crime laboratory accurately keep track of all the evidence going in and out of its testing facility? A single piece of lost evidence could mean the difference between a solved—or forever unsolved—crime story.

Challenge

While the Silicon Valley is not known for its high crime rates, it is known for its leadership in technology. To that end, Santa Clara County recently opened a new $75.5 million, state-of-the-art crime laboratory in the Silicon Valley. With a staff of more than 60 professional crime solvers, this laboratory examines thousands of pieces of criminal evidence coming in from local, state and federal agencies such as area sheriff, police and fire departments as well as probation officers and the courts.

This 90,000 sq. ft., four-story complex is equipped to handle digital evidence, perform DNA typing, fingerprint analysis, ballistics and firearms testing, toxicology and drug testing, and assist with crime scene processing. The crime laboratory receives more than 35,000 pieces of evidence each year, according to Benny Del Re, Crime Laboratory Director.

This new laboratory replaces a decades-old crime laboratory that was spread out among three separate buildings in Santa Clara County. In the old laboratory, much of the equipment being used to evaluate evidence was antiquated, slow and unreliable, which resulted in a backlog of cases as high as 600 at times, with a turnaround time for evidence as long as 35 days. The old laboratory used a manual bar code scanning system to track the flow of evidence.

Solution

To provide ultimate efficiency in the crime laboratory, Laboratory Director Del Re worked with system integrator CIBER, Inc. to develop a fully integrated solution that includes a floor-to-floor, passive RFID evidence tracking system. Using RFID solutions from Alien Technology, the laboratory can track and monitor the movement of evidence as criminalists and other staff members check it out of storage in the property lockers and take it to the various laboratories for testing.

"We wanted to find a better way than bar coding to track evidence as it traveled through the four story laboratory," says Del Re. "Our concern is knowing where any one particular piece of evidence is at any one time, and who it had been assigned to." The CIBER team, familiar with the benefits of RFID in supply chain management, recommended using Alien RFID solutions to Del Re before the laboratory was even completed.

"We wanted to track the movement of evidence throughout the building in an innovative, efficient way," says Del Re. "We are breaking ground by using RFID. We're the first laboratory in the U.S. to do that."

Results

With the RFID system, the laboratory tracks movement of all evidence throughout its entire evaluation cycle. First, the evidence is brought in by law enforcement agencies that use a Web-based system to log it into the crime database. The RFID tracking system works alongside the Laboratory Information Management System (LIMS) already in use at the Santa Clara Crime Laboratory.

Once the physical evidence is at the laboratory, Del Re's team attaches an Alien RFID Squiggle tag as well as a bar code to the evidence before it enters the first floor property room. The bar code is a backup system to the RFID. With both technologies in place, the laboratory has 100 percent accuracy in evidence tracking.

"Using RFID and bar coding is the best of both worlds," says Del Re. "We have the efficiency and accuracy of RFID. With criminal evidence, we can't afford mistakes."

The team uses two different-sized RFID tags: A small one for evidence such as blood vials and a standard tag for all other evidence. The tag is affixed to all kinds of substances, including plastic bags containing tiny pieces of evidence as well as blood vial trays and even automobiles. It will need to withstand elements such as the below freezing temperatures in cold storage.

The building currently has seven Alien RFID 9650 readers at checkpoints on every floor, located inside the property room and near the elevators. The staff and the evidence technicians use the checkpoints to confirm the evidence inventory as they check it out, move it to the laboratory, and return it to the property lockers. The tracking system reads the RFID identifier and acknowledges when it leaves the evidence locker on any given floor. By using RFID to monitor the "chain of custody" of the evidence, the laboratory can improve the efficiency and quality of tracking.

Benefits and Next Steps

The new laboratory equipment, along with its more efficient RFID tracking system will result in a quantifiable increase in process turn-around time. Multiple law enforcement agencies will also be able to access the evidence database, allowing the linking of evidence from crimes across different jurisdictions.

And at any given time, the laboratory can locate a single piece of criminal evidence.

CHAPTER 7

Conclusions

What's Next?

To this point in the book we have mostly discussed the current state of RFID. So now the question is what does the future hold for this technology? RFID still faces some legal challenges, especially in terms of privacy concerns. Cultural norms will continue to be challenged and new norms will eventually be established. Among the major technological issues that will affect all RFID deployments are the introduction of intelligent readers, changes in global standards, improvements in tags, improvements in software capabilities, and reductions in the cost of tags. An intelligent RFID reader eliminates the need for middleware, which will result in a substantial reduction in the cost of RFID technology. The cost reductions will be realized from eliminating the need to purchase an out-of-the box middleware solution or hiring a programmer to create that link. Some companies such as Alien Software Corporation have created software that will extend the capabilities of an RFID reader. The work currently going on to reduce the cost of the UHF passive tag will reduce the ongoing cost for implementing an RFID system. The in-transit visibility (ITV) software is described by Alien as a reader toolkit that will capture information such as tag location, direction of movement, and speed of movement.[1]

While the future of RFID technology is not as clear as one would like in terms of uses, there are some indications of RFID's potential for both extensions of current uses and innovative new uses. The Canadian and U.S. governments both indicate that there is a need to begin training employees in RFID technology now because there will be a shortage of people with those necessary skills in the future.[2] The future for RFID is bright and the market is growing rapidly with forecasts for RFID technology becoming a $4 billion industry by 2019.

Examples of Extensions of Current Uses

Education

As previously discussed, some school districts are already using RFID technology to track students both during transit and inside of buildings. Schools in the future will most likely use RFID asset management to track high-value items, such as laptops, sports equipment, and musical instruments. If the cost of implementation continues its downward trend, even low-cost pieces of equipment are more likely to be tracked. Schools will potentially be able to track books, cafeteria trays, art supplies, and other associated supplies. Schools would be able to immediately verify that students were picked up by an authorized person by verifying the authorized person's identification via a database with biometric information. Additionally if a student is riding a bus or walking to school, parents will be able to verify the students' safe arrival because attendance can be taken as the student enters the building and the record automatically placed in a database for parents to access. Schools will be able to match students with any special requirements. For example, as a child moves through a lunch line with their RFID enabled student identification, the

Figure 7.1. Sports equipment tagged with RFID.

Photograph courtesy of the Sower Business Technology Laboratory, College of Business Administration, Sam Houston State University.

system will be able to alert both the student and the adults monitoring the system if the student picks an item that could cause an allergic reaction. Student badges may be able to act as payment cards for students purchasing lunches in the cafeteria and snacks at the vending machines. Not only could it act as a payment card, but it may actually give parents more control over what the students purchase in order to prevent them from buying foods they may be allergic to and to restrict the amount of junk food they eat.[3]

Health Care

Several hospitals are already using RFID in the operating room to track surgical instruments and sponges, and in some cases the technology is used to track medical personnel within the hospital. Many more hospitals use RFID to track assets and minimize medication errors. But there are many other potential extensions in the health care industry. RFID asset management will most likely be extended in the health care industry to include emergency responders. In a catastrophic event, RFID could be used to manage assets outside the hospital, such as medical personnel and ambulances, to ensure they are correctly directed to the location where they are needed most. In addition, the technology will allow coordinators to know where all their assets are so they can best coordinate rescue efforts.

The health care industry will very likely continue to expand its use of RFID. For example, RFID matching will be used to match patients to their medical records. The patient will wear a wristband and the attending medical personnel will have a handheld computer with reader capability. This technique will match the wristband with the patient's medical records and the information can immediately be placed into that patient's records. During a catastrophic event, medical personnel could use wristbands to prioritize the patients for medical treatment using this same matching process. Medical personnel would be able to use RFID matching and RFID asset management to identify the victims that most urgently need care and coordinate the evacuation of those patients by locating assets such as ambulances to immediately take them to a medical facility. The emergency-management personnel would then be able to identify the nearest hospital with an available room.[4] In the future,

RFID could control access to surgical units and deny access if the medical personnel are not properly scrubbed or equipped to enter. In addition, RFID asset tracking can be used to track surgical tools to ensure that they have been sterilized, potentially lowering the incidence of infections contracted in an operating room.

Pharmaceuticals

In the pharmaceutical industry, RFID provides value to pharmacies in terms of authenticity, order confirmation, process transparency, lot validation, date-code validation, and patient safety.[5] Extensions for the use of RFID technology can be anticipated as well. For example, for patient safety, refrigerators are being equipped to monitor the temperature of medication to make sure that it is maintained at designated levels. In addition, the medication could be tracked for usage to ensure that the patient is taking the correct dosage at the correct time (J. Baker, Venture Research, Inc., interview with author, November 9, 2010).

Retail

The retail industry has certainly been one of the early adopters of RFID technology. While retailers are currently using the technology for inventory management and security, the focus for the future will be customer responsiveness. For example, retailers could use RFID to identify customers as they enter stores and malls. RFID's potential in this area is seemingly endless. A person might be able to go to the mall and, upon entry, use an identification card that would trigger the reader to pull up the customer's information in a database. The person would be directed to the parking space closest to their favorite stores. Grocery shopping could be made easier with shopping carts that are equipped with RFID. As an item is placed in the shopping cart, the price and tax are displayed. Customized advertisements for other items could be displayed to entice shoppers. Shoppers would be able to check out at the cart and then be on their way. Shopping for apparel will also change with the use of RFID. For example, a mirror equipped with the technology could partially eliminate the need for dressing rooms because the image in the mirror will reflect the customer in the clothing selected.[6]

Manufacturing

While RFID is being used for inventory management and security in manufacturing, that use has yet to become widespread. As the technology becomes more commonplace in manufacturing, it will be integrated into processes to add greater visibility, reduce bottlenecks, and produce higher-quality products. Companies will seek out supply chain partners that are RFID compatible for greater visibility in the supply chain. As discussed earlier, when coupled with an ERP system, RFID will provide near real-time information. Supply chains utilizing RFID will be able to divert supplies to where they are critically needed while keeping other supply chain members informed of the location of their products.[7]

While these potential extensions of RFID are not exhaustive, they are examples of how the technology will continue to grow in the future. Some of these extended uses are under way now, while some are a few years out. Now we need to take a look at some of the potential paradigm-shifting uses of the technology.

Examples of Potential New Uses in the Future

Traffic Flow

Researchers are forecasting the use of RFID in and along highways and with intermodal transportation.[8] While the use of RFID to pay highway tolls and monitor products as they move from place to place is not new, the use of the technology to navigate vehicles is. RFID could be used to reroute traffic when there is congestion and could be combined with sensors to identify dangers, such as sudden stops. It could even help eliminate the need for traffic control signs by automatically controlling the vehicle.

Smart Cane

The Smart Cane is a product for visually impaired people. Sensors are combined with RFID technology to enable the visually impaired to navigate safely via a navigational system. A speaker on the equipment alerts the users when there is an obstacle and navigates the individual around the obstacles. As the creators state, its use is limited now, but it has tremendous potential for the future.[9]

Inventory Management

We have all been to our local stores and malls during inventory time and seen the number of employees needed to accomplish the task. In the future, item-level RFID tagging could be integrated with an autonomous mobile robot to undertake that formidable task. IBM has recently received a patent on such a concept. RFID can reduce the amount of labor required to perform tasks while also improving accuracy. Arguments will be made that the system is eliminating jobs, and that may be true; however, companies might choose to redirect their resources to other areas of the business, resulting in no loss of jobs. But even if true, the jobs being eliminated are tedious and subject to error. The argument can also be made that this RFID technology would provide better jobs in producing and maintaining the robotic systems and also increase worker productivity.

Job Costing

Another advance is in job costing. As previously mentioned, RFID technology can be used to track not only the supplies used on a job but also the number of hours an employee actually spends working on the job. By providing a means of automatically providing near real-time information, this use of RFID should lead to more accurate job costing and higher productivity. However, employees may be uncomfortable with their employers tracking their movements.[10] This is a cultural issue rather than a technological one that will have to be appropriately addressed in order for the system to function properly.

Conclusions

Throughout this book we have given examples of how RFID technology is currently being used. Although RFID has been around for a long time, this is the dawn of a new industry. It is up to us to decide how the technology will be regulated and used. We have to analyze the benefits of RFID and weigh them against the costs. We have to use our ingenuity to find new uses for the technology to improve the way that we live and do business. The time is right for creative and innovative people to make dramatic improvements using RFID. What are you waiting for?

APPENDIX

RFID Standards

List of SC17 Documents*

ISO 8484 Magnetic stripes on savings books

ISO/IEC 10373-1 Test methods—General

ISO/IEC 10373-2 Test methods—Magnetic strip technologies

ISO/IEC 7810 Identification cards—Physical characteristics

ISO/IEC 7811-1 Identification cards—Recording technique—Embossing

ISO/IEC 7811-2 Identification cards—Recording technique—Magnetic stripe

ISO/IEC 7811-3 Identification cards—Recording technique—Location of embossed characters

ISO/IEC 7811-4 Identification cards—Recording technique—Location of tracks 1 and 2

ISO/IEC 7811-5 Identification cards—Recording technique—Location of track 3

ISO/IEC 7811-6 Identification cards—Recording technique—Magnetic stripe—High coercivity

ISO/IEC 15457-1 Identification cards—Thin flexible cards—Physical characteristics, magnetic recording techniques, test methods—Part 1: Physical Characteristics

ISO/IEC 15457-2 Identification cards—Thin flexible cards—Physical characteristics, magnetic recording techniques, test methods—Part 2: Magnetic recording techniques

ISO/IEC 15457-3 Identification cards—Thin flexible cards—Physical characteristics, magnetic recording techniques, test methods—Part 3: Test methods

---

* SC17 is a subcommittee of the ISO/IEC Joint Technical Committee on Information Technology.

ISO/IEC 7501-1 Identification cards—Machine-readable travel documents—Part 1: Machine-readable passport

ISO/IEC 7501-2 Identification cards—Machine-readable travel documents—Part 2: Machine readable visas

ISO/IEC 7501-3 Identification cards—Machine-readable travel documents—Official travel documents

NP 14543 Identification cards—Machine-readable travel documents—Machine-readable travel cards with coexistent technologies

ISO 7816-1 Identification cards—Integrated circuit(s) cards with contacts—Part 1: Physical characteristics.

ISO 7816-2 Identification cards—Integrated circuit(s) cards with contacts—Part 2: Dimensions and location of the contacts

ISO 7816-3 Identification cards—Integrated circuit(s) cards with contacts—Part 3: Electronic signals and transmission protocols

ISO/IEC 7816-4 Identification cards—Integrated circuit(s) cards with contacts—Part 4: Interindustry commands for interchange

ISO/IEC 7816-4/AM1 Impact of secure messaging on APDE structures

ISO/IEC 7816-5 Identification cards—Integrated circuit(s) cards with contacts—Part 5: Registration system for applications in IC Cards

ISO/IEC 7816-5/AM1 AM1: Proposal for a set of registered application provider identifiers (RIDs)

ISO/IEC 7816-6 Identification cards—Integrated circuit(s) cards with contacts—Part 6: Interindustry data elements

Defect Report ISO/IEC 7816-6 Technical corrigenda

ISO/IEC 7816-6/AM1 IC Manufacturer registration

ISO/IEC 7816-7 Identification cards—Integrated circuit(s) cards with contacts—Part 7: Interindustry commands for Structured Card Query Language (SCQL)

ISO/IEC 7816-8 Identification cards—Integrated circuit(s) cards with contacts—Part 8: Security architecture and related inter-industry commands

ISO/IEC 7816-9 Identification cards—Integrated circuit(s) cards with contacts—Part 9: Enhanced interindustry commands

ISO/IEC 7816-10 Identification cards—Integrated circuit(s) cards with contacts Part 10: Electronic signals and answer to reset for synchronous cards

ISO/IEC 7816-11 Identification cards—Integrated circuit(s) cards with contacts—Part 11: Framework for dynamic handling of multiple applications in integrated circuit cards

ISO/IEC 15460 Identification cards—Integrated circuit(s) cards with contacts—Integrated circuits with voltages lower than 3 volts

ISO/IEC 18020 Identification cards—Integrated circuit(s) cards with contacts—Personal verification through biometric methods in integrated circuit cards

ISO/IEC 10373-3 Test methods—Integrated circuit cards

ISO/IEC 7812-1: 1993 Identification cards—Identification of issuers—Part 1: Numbering system

ISO/IEC 7812-2: 1993 Identification cards—Identification of issuers—Part 2: Application and registration procedures

ISO/IEC 7813 Financial transaction cards

ISO/IEC 10536-1 Identification cards—Contactless integrated circuit(s) cards—Part 1: Physical characteristics.

ISO/IEC 10536-2 Identification cards—Contactless integrated circuit(s) cards—Part 2: Dimensions and location of coupling areas

ISO/IEC 10536-3 Identification cards—Contactless integrated circuit(s) cards—Part 3: Electronic signals and reset procedures

ISO/IEC 10536-4 Identification cards—Contactless integrated circuit(s) cards—Part 4: Answer to reset and transmission protocols

ISO/IEC 14443-1 Identification cards—Contactless integrated circuit(s) cards—Proximity integrated circuit(s) cards—Part 1: Physical characteristics

ISO/IEC 14443-2 Identification cards—Contactless integrated circuit(s) cards—Proximity integrated circuit(s) cards—Part 2: Radio frequency interface

ISO/IEC 14443-3 Identification cards—Contactless integrated circuit(s) cards—Proximity integrated circuit(s) cards—Part 3: Initialization and anticollision

ISO/IEC 14443-4 Identification cards—Contactless integrated circuit(s) cards—Proximity integrated circuit(s) cards—Part 4: Transmission protocols

ISO/IEC 15693-1 Identification cards—Contactless integrated circuit(s) cards—Vicinity cards—Part 1: Physical characteristics

ISO/IEC 15693-2 Identification cards—Contactless integrated circuit(s) cards—Vicinity cards—Part 2: Air interface and initialization

ISO/IEC 15693-3 Identification cards—Contactless integrated circuit(s) cards—Vicinity cards—Part 3: Protocols

ISO/IEC 15693-4 Identification cards—Contactless integrated circuit(s) cards—Vicinity cards—Part 4: Registration of applications/issuers

ISO/IEC 10373-4 Test methods—Contactless integrated circuit cards

ISO/IEC 10373-6 Test methods—Proximity cards

ISO/IEC 10373-7 Test methods—Vicinity cards

ISO/IEC 11693 Identification cards—Optical memory cards

ISO/IEC 11694-1 Identification cards—Optical memory cards and devices—Linear recording method—Part 1: Physical characteristics

ISO/IEC 11694-2 Identification cards—Optical memory cards and devices—Linear recording method—Part 2: Dimensions and location of the accessible optical area

ISO/IEC 11694-2/DAM1 Optional card layout

ISO/IEC 11694-3 Identification cards—Optical memory cards and devices—Linear recording method—Part 3: Optical properties and characteristics

ISO/IEC 11694-4 Identification cards—Optical memory cards and devices—Linear recording method—Part 4: Logical data structures

ISO/IEC 10373-5 Test methods—Optical memory cards

ISO/IEC 18013 Identification cards—Motor vehicle license

Standards Applicable to RFID That Are a Product of SC31*

ISO/IEC 15434 Transfer syntax for high-capacity ADC media

ISO/IEC 15459-1 Unique identifier for transport units—Part 1: Transport units

ISO/IEC 15459-2 Unique identifier for transport units—Part 2: Registration procedures

ISO/IEC 15459-3 Unique identifier for transport units—Part 3: Common rules

ISO/IEC 15459-4 Unique identifier for transport units—Part 4: Unique items

ISO/IEC 15459-5 Unique identifier for transport units—Part 5: Returnable transport items (RTIs)

ISO/IEC 15459-6 Unique identifier for transport units—Part 6: Product groupings

ISO/IEC 15459-7 Unique identifiers—Part 7: Unique identification of product packaging

ISO/IEC 15459-8 Unique identifiers—Part 8: Grouping of transport items

ISO/IEC 15961 RFID for item management—Data protocol: Application interface

ISO/IEC 15961 revision

- Data protocol—Part 1: Application interface
- Data protocol—Part 2: Registration of RFID data constructs
- Data protocol—Part 3: RFID data constructs
- Data protocol—Part 4: Application interface commands for battery assist and sensor functionality

ISO/IEC 15962 RFID for item management—Data protocol: Data encoding rules and logical memory functions

ISO/IEC 15962 revision RFID for item management—Data protocol: Data encoding rules and logical memory functions

---

* ISO/IEC JTC 1/SC31 is responsible for producing standards in automatic identification and data capture techniques.

ISO/IEC 15963 RFID for item management—Unique identification of RF tag

ISO/IEC 18000 See full details—Information technology AIDC techniques—RFID for item management—Air interface

- 18000-1 Part 1–Generic parameters for the air interface for globally accepted frequencies
- 18000-2 Part 2–Parameters for air interface communications below 135 kHz
- 18000-3 Part 3–Parameters for air interface communications at 13.56 MHz
- 18000-4 Part 4–Parameters for air interface communications at 2.45 GHz
- 18000-6 Part 6–Parameters for air interface communications at 860–960 MHz
- 18000-7 Part 7–Parameters for air interface communications at 433 MHz

ISO/IEC 18001 RFID for item management—Application requirements profiles (ARP)

ISO/IEC 18046 RFID tag and interrogator performance test methods

ISO/IEC 18046 revision RFID tag and interrogator performance test methods

- Part 1: Test methods for system performance
- Part 2: Test methods for interrogator performance
- Part 3: Test methods for tag performance

ISO/IEC 18047 RFID device conformance test methods, split to mirror ISO/IEC 18000

- 18047-1 Part 1–Not available
- 18047-2 Part 2–Parameters for air interface communications below 135 kHz
- 18047-3 Part 3–Parameters for air interface communications at 13.56 MHz
- 18047-4 Part 4–Parameters for air interface communications at 2.45 GHz
- 18047-5 Part 5–Not available

- 18047-6 Part 6–Parameters for air interface communications at 860–960 MHz
- 18047-7 Part 7–Parameters for air interface communications at 433 MHz

ISO/IEC 19762 Information technology AIDC techniques—
Harmonized vocabulary
- Part 1: General terms related to AIDC
- Part 2: Optically readable media (ORM)
- Part 3: Radio frequency identification (RFID)
- Part 4: Conceptual relationship between terms
- Part 5: Locating systems

ISO/IEC 24710 Information technology, automatic identification and data capture techniques—Radio frequency
identification for item management—Elementary tag license
plate functionality for ISO/IEC 18000 air interface definitions

ISO/IEC 24729 Information technology—Radio frequency iden-
tification for item management—Implementation guidelines
- Part 1: RFID-enabled labels.
- Part 2: Recyclability of RF tags
- Part 3: RFID interrogator/antenna installation
- Part 4: RFID guideline on tag data security

ISO/IEC 24730 Real-time locating systems (RTLS)
- Part 1: Application program interface (API)
- Part 2: 2.4 GHz air interface protocol
- Part 3: 433 MHz air interface protocol
- Part 4: Global locating systems (GLS)
- Part 5: 2.4 GHz personal area network (PAN) air interface

ISO/IEC 24753 Information technology—Automatic identification and data capture techniques—Radio frequency
identification (RFID) for item management—Air interface
commands for battery assist and sensor functionality

ISO/IEC 24769 Information technology—Automatic identification and data capture techniques—Real-time locating systems (RTLS)—RTLS device conformance test methods

ISO/IEC 24770 Information technology—Automatic identification and data capture techniques—Real-time locating systems (RTLS)—RTLS device performance test methods

ISO/IEC 24791 Information technology—Automatic identification and data capture techniques—Radio frequency identification (RFID) for item management—Software system infrastructure
- Part 1: Device management
- Part 2: Data management
- Part 3: Application management
- Part 4: Application interface
- Part 5: Device interface
- Part 6: Security

ISO/IEC 29143 Information technology—Automatic identification and data capture techniques—Air interface specification for mobile RFID interrogator

ISO/IEC 29160 Information technology—Automatic identification and data capture techniques—RFID emblem

ISO/IEC 29167 Information technology—Automatic identification and data capture techniques—Air interface for file management and security services for RFID

ISO/IEC 29172 Information technology—Automatic identification and data capture techniques—Mobile item identification and management—Reference architecture for mobile AIDC services

ISO/IEC 29173 Information technology—Automatic identification and data capture techniques—Mobile item identification and management—Mobile RFID interrogator device protocol

ISO/IEC 29174 Information technology—Automatic identification and data capture techniques—Mobile item identification and management—UII scheme and encoding format for mobile AIDC services

ISO/IEC 29175 Information technology—Automatic identification and data capture techniques—Mobile item identification

and management—Application data structure and encoding
format for mobile AIDC services

ISO/IEC 29176 Information technology—Automatic identification and data capture techniques—Mobile item identification
and management—Consumer privacy-protection protocol for
mobile AIDC services

ISO/IEC 29177 Information technology—Automatic identification and data capture techniques—Mobile item identification and
management—Object Directory Service for mobile AIDC services

ISO/IEC 29178 Information technology—Automatic identification and data capture techniques—Mobile item identification
and management—Service broker for mobile AIDC services

ISO/IEC 29179 Information technology—Automatic identification and data capture techniques—Mobile item identification and
management—Mobile AIDC application programming interface

ETSI

EN 302 208 Radio frequency identification equipment operating
in the band 865 MHz to 868 MHz with power levels up to 2 W

TR 102 313 Frequency-agile generic short-range devices using
listen-before-transmit (LBT)

Technical Report

TR 101 445 Short-range devices (SRD) intended for operation
in the 862 MHz to 870 MHz band; System reference document for radio frequency identification (RFID) equipment

EN 300 330 Short-range devices (SRD); Technical characteristics
and test methods for radio equipment in the frequency range
9 kHz to 25 MHz and inductive loop systems in the frequency
range 9 kHz to 30 MHz

EN 300 220 Short-range devices (SRD); Radio equipment to
be used in the 25 MHz to 1 000 MHz frequency range with
power levels ranging up to 500 mW

EN 300 440 Radio equipment to be used in the 1 GHz to 40
[61.5] GHz frequency range

EN 302 208 Radio frequency identification equipment operating
in the band 865 MHz to 868 MHz with power levels up to 2 W

EN 301 489 part 1 and part 3 Electromagnetic compatibility
(EMC) standard for radio equipment and services

TR 102 649-1 Technical characteristics of RFID in the UHF
band; System reference document for radio frequency identification (RFID) equipment;

Part 1: RFID equipment operating in the range from 865 MHz to
868 MHz

TR 102 449 Telecommunications and Internet converged services and protocols for advanced networking (TISPAN)

Overview of Radio Frequency Identification (RFID) Tags in the Telecommunications Industry

TR 102 436 Short-range devices (SRD) intended for operation
in the band 865 MHz to 868 MHz

Guidelines for the Installation and Commissioning of Radio Frequency Identification (RFID) Equipment at UHF

TS 102 562 Improved spectrum efficiency for RFID in the UHF
band

Guidelines for Securing RFID Systems

NIST Special Publication 800-98 Guidelines for securing radio
frequency identification (RFID) systems

ISO/IEC TR24729-4 Information technology—Radio frequency identification for item management—Implementation
guidelines—Part 4: Tag data security

ISO/IEC 24791-5 Information technology—Radio frequency
identification device conformance test methods

Notes

Chapter 1

1. Intermec Technologies Corporation (2010).
2. Fraley and Snider (n.d.).
3. Zebra Technologies Corp. (2011b).

Chapter 2

1. Research and Markets (2011, February 21).
2. "Cloud computing" (2007, December).
3. Grossman (2010).
4. Allen et al. (2009), pp. 325–332.
5. Alien Technology Corporation (2008c).
6. Alien Technology Corporation (2008c).
7. Drori (n.d.).
8. Srivastava (2010), pp. 289–307.
9. Alien Technology Corporation (2008c).
10. Alien Technology Corporation (2008c).
11. Drori (n.d.).
12. "A summary" (n.d.).
13. Drori (n.d.).

Chapter 3

1. Bacheldor (2009, March 4).
2. Bacheldor (2009, March 4).
3. Karygiannis et al. (2007), p. 3-2.
4. Karygiannis et al. (2007), p. 3-3.
5. Karygiannis et al. (2007), p. 3-3.
6. Karygiannis et al. (2007), p. 3-3.
7. Karygiannis et al. (2007), p. 3-3.
8. Karygiannis et al. (2007), p. 3-4.
9. Karygiannis et al. (2007), p. 3-5.
10. Karygiannis et al. (2007), p. 3-5.
11. Swedberg (2011, April 21).

12. Friedlos (2011, May 17).

13. Violino (2008, October 20).

14. Wessel (2009, October 14).

15. "Improving RFID"(2009, August 3).

16. "RFID technology now" (2010).

17. "Improving RFID" (2009, August 3).

18. ThingMagic. (2009, April 21).

19. Alien Technology Corporation (2008b).

20. Intermec Technologies Corporation (2010).

21. Jahed and Hossain (2009).

22. Impinj, Inc. (2009).

23. Bacheldor (2007).

24. Bacheldor (2007, June 19).

25. discoverrfid.org (n.d.).

26. Sakr (2011, February 6).

27. Rohrlich (2010, December 15).

28. "China taps" (2007, April 7).

29. Process Data Control Corporation (2010).

30. Bacheldor (2008, July 29).

31. Impinj, Inc. (2010).

32. Fraley and Snider (n.d.).

33. Fraley and Snider (n.d.).

34. Snider and Fraley (2007, March/April).

35. Fraley and Snider (n.d.).

36. Swedberg (2010, February 9).

37. Bacheldor (2008, August 21).

38. Baard (2005, April 12), p. 1.

39. Chabrow (2005, January 25).

40. Lopez (2010, October 20).

41. Radcliffe (2010, October 11).

42. Radcliffe (2010, October 11).

43. Noonan (2010).

44. O'Connor (2005, November 2).

45. Alien Technology Corporation (2008a).

46. Alien Technology Corporation (2008a).

47. Srivastava (2010), pp. 289–307.

48. United Parcel Service of America, Inc. (2005).

49. U.S. Department of Defense (2011).

50. Songini (2007, February 26).

51. "RFID technology" (2010, July 13).

52. Falken Secure Networks (2011).

53. Pisello (2006, August).

54. O'Brien (2004).
55. Sullivan (2005, October 10).
56. Schapranow (2009).
57. Roberti (2009, June 29).
58. MacManus (2010).
59. Johnson (2008, January 4).
60. Roberti (2004, June 18).
61. Gilbert (2005, July 8).
62. Lynch (2010, November 30).
63. Lynch (2010, November 30).
64. Savi Active RFID Tags (2011).
65. Bacheldor (2009, February 24).
66. Parker (2003).
67. Narcoe (2010).

Chapter 4

1. Karygiannis et al. (2007), p. 2-1.
2. Zelbst et al. (2010a).
3. Zelbst et al. (2010b).
4. Zelbst et al. (in press).
5. Zelbst et al. (2010b).
6. H.B. 1134 (Tex. 2011).
7. "House of cards" (2011), p. 23.
8. Bowser (2009).
9. "House of cards" (2011), p. 23.
10. Strauch (2008, March 19).
11. Zebra Technologies Corp. (2011a).
12. Goldman and Crawford (2004, January 6).
13. Trebilcock (2011, January 23).
14. Myers (2011, February 3).
15. Myers (2011, February 3).

Chapter 5

1. TIBCO (2006).
2. TIBCO (2006).
3. Fleming (2010, September 13), p. 7.
4. Sower and Sower (2011), pp. 119–121.
5. Omni-ID (2009).

Chapter 7

1. Alien Technology Corporation (n.d.).
2. Songini (2007, May 31).
3. Wasserman (2010, March 21).
4. Roberti (2008, September 15).
5. Alien Technology Corporation (2009).
6. Roberti (2009, December 1).
7. Zaino (2010, January 26).
8. Orr (2007, June).
9. Whitney (2009, August 4).
10. Bellah et al. (in press).

References

Alien Technology Corporation. (2008a). RFID revitalizes the vending machine business with deli-fresh food in a self-service checkout. Retrieved from http://www.alientechnology.com/docs/CS_Freedom.pdf

Alien Technology Corporation. (2008b). RFID for passive asset tracking: Delivering process improvements and cost savings through automatic asset tracking. Retrieved from http://www.alientechnology.com/docs/applications/SBAssetTracking.pdf

Alien Technology Corporation. (2008c). *RFID now!* Dayton, OH: RFID Solution Center.

Alien Technology Corporation. (2009). Pharmaceutical shifts towards UHF RFID for savings. Retrieved from http://www.alientechnology.com/docs/WP_UHF_RFIDPharmaceutical.pdf

Alien Technology Corporation. (n.d.). *Intelligent Tag Radar*. Retrieved from http://www.alientechnology.com/readers/itr.php

Allen, M. L., Jaakkola, K., Nummila, K., & Seppä, H. (2009). Applicability of metallic nanoparticle inks in RFID applications. *IEEE Transactions on Components and Tracking Technologies 32*(2), 325–332.

Baard, M. (2005, April 12). Ridge says RFID boosts security. *Wired*. Retrieved from http://www.wired.com/print/politics/security/news/2005/04/67192

Bacheldor, B. (2007). Australian companies say pallet-tracking project proves RFID's mettle. *RFID Journal*. Retrieved from http://www.rfidjournal.com/article/view/3467

Bacheldor, B. (2007, June 19). Manufacturers propose tools to fight counterfeiting. *RFID Journal*. Retrieved from http://www.rfidjournal.com/article/view/3421

Bacheldor, B. (2008, July 29). Stanley bolsters RFID portfolio with VeriChip's ex-subsidiary. *RFID Journal*. Retrieved from http://www.rfidjournal.com/article/view/4219

Bacheldor, B. (2008, August 21). ADT expects RFID will reduce false alarms for home security. *RFID Journal*. Retrieved from http://www.rfidjournal.com/article/view/4274

Bacheldor, B. (2009, February 24). Hybrid tag includes active RFID, GPS, satellite and sensors. *RFID Journal*. Retrieved from http://www.rfidjournal.com/article/view/4635

Bacheldor, B. (2009, March 4). RFID, sensor technologies can build smarter supply chains, IBM says. *RFID Journal*. Retrieved from http://www.rfidjournal.com/article/view/4653

Bellah, J. C., Li, K., & Zelbst, P. J. (in press). Use of RFID technology for automatic job costing. *International Journal of Knowledge-Based Organizations*.

Bowser, D. (2009). RFID tag data security technical report based on guidance from AIM's RFID expert group is published by ISO. Association for Automatic Identification and Mobility. Retrieved July 18, 2011, from http://www.aimglobal.org/members/news/templates/template.aspx?articleid=3468&zoneid=1

Chabrow, E. (2005, January 25). Homeland Security to test RFID tags at U.S. borders. *Information Week*. Retrieved from http://www.informationweek.com/news/57703738

China taps into RFID for Olympics. (2007, April 17). *RFID News*. Retrieved from http://www.rfidnews.org/2007/04/17/china-taps-into-rfid-for-olympics

Cloud computing. (2007, December). *Search Cloud Computing*. Retrieved from http://searchcloudcomputing.techtarget.com/definition/cloud-computing

discoverrfid.org. (n.d.). Ensuring the authenticity of medicine. Retrieved from http://www.discoverrfid.org/what-is-possible/stay-healthy/fighting-counterfeiting.html

Drori, R. (n.d.). *RFID White Paper*. Rosh Ha'ayin, Israel: MTI Wireless Edge Ltd. Retrieved from http://www.mtiwe.com/page.aspx?parent=23&id=283&type=2

Falken Secure Networks. (2011). RFID enables real-time supply chain management. Retrieved from http://www.falkensecurenetworks.com/PDFs/0811_RFID_keeps_Canadian_Food_Supply-Chain_Safe.pdf

Fleming, E. (2010, September 13). RFID ROI: In-depth. *RFID Network*. Retrieved from http://rfid.net/best-practices/43-best-practices/144-rfid-roi-in-depth

Fraley, K., & Snider, P. (n.d.) RFID technology for downhole well applications. *Touch Gastroenterology*. Retrieved from http://www.touchgastroenterology.com/rfid-technology-downhole-well-applications?page=0%2C0

Friedlos, D. (2011, May 17). Korean warehouses deploy RFID-enhanced pick-to-light system. *RFID Journal*. Retrieved from http://www.rfidjournal.com/article/view/8428

Gilbert, A. (2005, July 8). Will RFID-guided robots rule the world? *ZDNet*. Retrieved from http://www.zdnet.com/news/will-rfid-guided-robots-rule-the-world/143615

Goldman, A., & Crawford, K. (2004, January 6). Five RFID myths exposed. *Wi-Fi Planet*. Retrieved from http://www.wi-fiplanet.com/tutorials/article.php/3296031/Five-RFID-Myths-Exposed.htm

Grossman, L. (2010). New RFID tag could mean the end of bar codes. *Science News*. Retrieved from http://www.wired.com/wiredscience/2010/03/rfid

H.B. 1134. 82nd Gen. Assem., Reg. Sess. (Tex. 2011). Retrieved from http://www.capitol.state.tx.us/BillLookup/History.aspx?LegSess=82R&Bill=HB1134

House of cards: Why your accounts are vulnerable to thieves. (2011). *Consumer Reports*, June 2011, 23–26.

Impinj, Inc. (2010). Monroe County cleans up with RFID. Impinj, Inc. Retrieved from http://www.impinj.com/applications/SubOneCol.aspx?id=3065

Impinj, Inc. (2009). RFID case study: Japan pallet rental. Impinj, Inc. Retrieved from http://www.impinj.com/Applications/Case_Studies.aspx

Improving RFID for oilfield operations. (2009, August 3). *Digital Energy Journal*. Retrieved from http://www.digitalenergyjournal.com/displaynews.php?NewsID =1011

Intermec Technologies Corporation. (2010). Mission Foods boosts asset control, increases inventory traceability with RFID technology. Retrieved from http://www.intermec.com/learning/content_library/case_studies/csMission2.aspx

Jahed, M. A., & Hossain, M. M. (2009). "Using radio frequency identification (RFID) technology to improve supply chain efficiency." *The Bangladesh Accountant*, October–December 2009.

Johnson, G. (2008, January 4). Integrating active RFID with ERP and legacy systems. *Toolbox.com*. Retrieved from http://it.toolbox.com/blogs/integrate-my -jde/integrating-active-rfid-with-erp-and-legacy-systems-21597

Karygiannis, T., Eydt, B., Barber, G., Bunn, L., & Phillips, T. (2007). *Guidelines for securing radio frequency identification (RFID) systems* (NIST Serial Publication 800–98). Gaithersburg, MD: National Institute of Standards and Technology.

Lopez, R. (2010, October 20). Four-year-old boy left on Plano school bus. *WFAA-TV*. Retrieved from http://www.wfaa.com/news/local/Child-Left-on -Bus-105368043.html

Lynch, K. (2010, November 30). Personal robotics advance with UHF RFID. *ThingMagic*. Retrieved from http://rfid.thingmagic.com/rfid-blog/bid/51637/ Personal-Robotics-Advance-with-UHF-RFID

MacManus, R. (2010, May 20). Sensor & RFID apps of the future, part 1. *ReadWriteWeb*. Retrieved from http://www.readwriteweb.com/archives/sensor_rfid _apps_of_the_future_part_1.php

Myers, W. (2011, February 3). RFID myths. *The Raco Pulse*. Retrieved from http://www.racoindustries.com/blog/post/RFID-Myths.aspx

Narcoe, J. (2010). RFID billboards to address consumers by name. *INFOWAR*. Retrieved from http://infowar.co/featured/rfid-billboards-to-address-consumers -by-name

Noonan, P. (2010, October 17). Safety afoot, via GPS, for Alzheimer's patients. *USA Weekend*, p. 4.

O'Brien, E. (2004, January 12). SAP introduces new RFID package. *SearchSAP*. Retrieved from http://searchsap.techtarget.com/news/944164/SAP-introduces -new-RFID-package

O'Connor, M. C. (2005, November 2). Vending machines accept RFID cards. *RFID Journal*. Retrieved from http://www.rfidjournal.com/article/view/1963

Omni-ID. (2009). High performance passive RFID tags: Best practices guide. *Omni-ID Limited*. Retrieved from http://www.omni-id.com/pdfs/RFID_Tag _Implementation_Testing_Deployment_Guide.pdf

Orr, V. (2007, June). Horizon lines introduces first intermodal RFID program to Alaska: Radio frequency identification to provide real-time shipment. *Alaska Business Monthly*. Retrieved from http://findarticles.com/p/articles/mi _hb5261/is_6_23/ai_n29357785

Parker, R. (2003, May 26). Implantable RFID and GPS devices. *FuturePundit*. Retrieved from http://www.futurepundit.com/archives/001299.html

Pisello, T. (2006, August). *Shrinking the supply chain expands the return: The ROI of RFID in the supply chain*. Orlando, FL: Alinean Press. Retrieved from http://www.motorola.com/web/Business/Solutions/Industry%20Solutions/ RFID%20Solutions/Documents/Static%20Flies/Alinean_ROI_WP_0917 _final.pdf?localeId=82

Process Data Control Corporation. (2010). Smart Band RFID wristbands combat counterfeiting at world-renowned SXSW festivals. Retrieved from http:// www.pdcorp.com/en-us/rfid-ent/case-study-sxsw.html

Radcliffe, J. (2010, October 11). Tracking devices used in school badges. *Houston Chronicle*. Retrieved from http://www.privacylives.com/houston-chronicle -tracking-devices-used-in-school-badges/2010/10/18

Research and Markets. (2011, February 21). Research and markets: Printed and chipless RFID forecasts, technologies & players 2011–2021. *Business Wire*. Retrieved from http://www.businesswire.com/news/home/20110221005718/ en/Research-Markets-Printed-Chipless-RFID-Forecasts-Technologies

RFID technology: Keeping track of DoD's stuff. (2010, July 13). *Defense Industry Daily*. Retrieved from http://www.defenseindustrydaily.com/?s=RFID+ technology%3A+Keeping+track+of+DoD%E2%80%99s+stuff

RFID technology now available for O & G industry. (2010, August 10). *Rigzone*. Retrieved from https://www.rigzone.com/news/article.asp?a_id=97220

Roberti, M. (2004, June 18). Navy revs up RFID sensors. *RFID Journal*. Retrieved from http://www.rfidjournal.com/article/view/990

Roberti, M. (2008, September 15). Use RFID to put the patient first. *RFID Journal*. Retrieved from http://www.rfidjournal.com/article/view/4322

Roberti, M. (2009, June 29). Bar-code technology is not cheaper than RFID. *RFID Journal*. Retrieved from http://www.rfidjournal.com/article/view/5005

Roberti, M. (2009, December 1). A family trip to the mall. *RFID Journal*. Retrieved from http://www.rfidjournal.com/article/view/7239

Rohrlich, J. (2010, December 15). The Bellagio gets robbed—but the house doesn't feel a thing. *Minyanville*. Retrieved from http://www.minyanville.com/articles/print.php?a=31714

Sakr, S. (2011, February 6). RFID: Radio tags set to combat counterfeiters. *BBC News*. Retrieved from http://www.bbc.co.uk/news/business-12358919

Savi Active RFID Tags. (2011). Savi Technology. Retrieved from http://www.savi.com/products/rfid/rfid-tags.php

Schapranow, M. (2009). RFID—real-life experiences at the Hasso Plattner Institute. Lecture given at the SAP Sapphire 2009 Conference.

Snider, P., & Fraley, K. (2007, March/April). Marathon, partners adapt RFID technology for downhole drilling, completion applications. *Downhole Tools*.

Songini, M. L. (2007, February 26). Procter & Gamble: Wal-Mart RFID effort effective. *Computerworld*. Retrieved from http://www.computerworld.com/s/article/284160/Procter_Gamble_Wal_Mart_RFID_Effort_Effective

Songini, M. L. (2007, May 31). Survey: RFID adoption hobbled by lack of trained staff. *Computerworld*. Retrieved from http://www.computerworld.com/s/article/9022359/Survey_RFID_adoption_hobbled_by_lack_of_trained_staff

Sower, V., & Sower, C. (2011). *Better business decisions using cost modeling*. New York: Business Expert Press.

Srivastava, B. (2010). Critical management issues for implementing RFID in supply chain management. *International Journal of Manufacturing Technology and Management 21*(3/4), 289–307.

Strauch, A. (2008, March 19). RFID physical security and privacy in retail. *RFID Solutions Online*. Retrieved from http://www.rfidsolutionsonline.com/article.mvc/RFID-Physical-Security-And-Privacy-In-Retail-0001

Sullivan, L. (2005, October 10). RFID implementation challenges persist, all this time later. *Information Week*. Retrieved from http://www.informationweek.com/news/171203904

A summary of RFID standards. (n.d.). *RFID Journal*. Retrieved from http://www.rfidjournal.com/article/view/1335

Swedberg, C. (2010, February 9). Vancouver hotel tracks an Olympic quantity of washable items. *RFID Journal*. Retrieved from http://www.rfidjournal.com/article/view/7381

Swedberg, C. (2011, April 21). Sumitomo Electric Lightwave boosts productivity in its warehouse. *RFID Journal*. Retrieved from http://www.rfidjournal.com/article/view/8373

ThingMagic. (2009, April 21). ThingMagic RFID enables asset tracking for Greenville Hospital. Retrieved from http://www.thingmagic.com/press-room/27-press-releases/245-thingmagic-rfid-enables-asset-tracking-for-greenville-hospital

TIBCO. (2006). TIBCO RFID implementation and integration solutions. Retrieved from http://www.tibco.com/multimedia/ds-rfid-solutions_tcm8-2413.pdf

Trebilcock, B. (2011, January 23). 2011 automatic data capture (ADC) user survey. *Modern Materials Handling*. Retrieved from http://www.mmh.com/article/2011_automatic_data_capture_adc_user_survey

United Parcel Service of America, Inc. (2005). *Demystifying in the supply chain: An overview of the promise and pitfalls*. Retrieved from http://www.ups-scs.com/solutions/white_papers/wp_RFID.pdf?srch_pos=3&srch_phr=Demystifying+the+supply+chain

U.S. Department of Defense. (2011). *Radio frequency identification (RFID)s*. Retrieved from https://kb.defense.gov/app/answers/detail/a_id/483/~/radio-frequency-identification-(rfid)s

Violino, B. (2008, October 20). Maternity apparel maker gives birth to smart displays in stores. *RFID Journal*. Retrieved from http://www.rfidjournal.com/article/view/4390

Wasserman, E. (2010, March 21). RFID 2030: Home and education. *RFID Journal*. Retrieved from http://www.rfidjournal.com/article/view/7413/5

Wessel, R. (2009, October 14). Lisbon Airport ups throughput with RFID baggage system. *RFID Journal*. Retrieved from http://www.rfidjournal.com/article/view/5302

Whitney, L. (2009, August 4). Smart cane to help blind navigate. *CNET*. Retrieved from http://news.cnet.com/8301-17938_105-10302499-1.html

Zaino, J. (2010, January 26). RFID 2030: Retail and manufacturing. *RFID Journal*. Retrieved from http://www.rfidjournal.com/article/view/7324/7

Zebra Technologies Corp. (2011a). *How bar codes and RFID deliver value to manufacturing and distribution* (WP1026566). Lincolnshire, IL: Zebra Technologies. Retrieved from http://www.zebra.com/id/zebra/na/en/documentlibrary/whitepapers/how_bar_codes_and.File.tmp/QP1026566.pdf

Zebra Technologies Corp. (2011b). *Unchaining the value of RFID for unmatched flexibility and fast ROI* (P1036571). Lincolnshire, IL: Zebra Technologies. Retrieved from http://www.zebra.com/id/zebra/na/en/index/resource_library/white_papers_abstracts.abstract.L2NvbnRlbnQvemVicmEvbmEvZW4vZG9jdW1lbnRsaWJyYXJ5L3doaXRlcGFwZXJzL3JmaWRfY2xc2VkX2xvb3A-.html

Zelbst, P., Green, K., & Sower, V. (2010a). Impact of RFID technology utilization on supply chain performance. *Management Research Review, 33*(10), 994–1004.

Zelbst, P., Green, K., Sower, V., & Baker, G. (2010b). RFID utilization and information sharing: The impact on supply chain performance. *Journal of Business & Industrial Marketing, 25*(8), 582–589.

Zelbst, P., K. Green, V. Sower, & R. Abshire. (2011) "Impact of RFID technology utilization on organizational agility." *Journal of Computer Information Systems, 52*(1), 24-33.

Index

Announcing the Business Expert Press Digital Library

Concise E-books Business Students
Need for Classroom and Research

This book can also be purchased in an e-book collection by your library as

- a one-time purchase,
- that is owned forever,
- allows for simultaneous readers,
- has no restrictions on printing,
- can be downloaded as PDFs from within the library community.

Our digital library collections are a great solution to beat the rising cost of textbooks. E-books can be loaded into their course management systems or onto students' e-book readers.

The **Business Expert Press** digital libraries are very affordable, with no obligation to buy in future years.

For more information, please visit **www.businessexpertpress.com/librarians**. To set up a trial in the United States, please contact **Sheri Dean** at sheri.dean@globalpress.com; for all other regions, contact **Nicole Lee** at nicole.lee@igroupnet.com.

OTHER TITLES IN OUR SUPPLY AND OPERATIONS MANAGEMENT COLLECTION
Collection Editor: **Steven Nahmias**, *Santa Clara University*

- *A Primer on Negotiating Corporate Purchase Contracts,* by Patrick Penfield
- *Production Line Efficiency,* by Sabry Shaaban
- *Transforming US Army Supply Chains,* by Greg Parlier
- *Design, Analysis and Optimization of Supply Chains,* by William, R. Killingsworth
- *Supply Chain Planning and Analytics,* by Gerald Feigin
- *Supply-Chain Survival in the Age of Globalization,* by James A. Pope
- *Better Business Decisions Using Cost Modeling,* by Victor E. Sower and Christopher Sower
- *Supply Chain Risk Management,* by David Olson
- *Leading and Managing the Lean Management Process,* by Gene Fliedner
- *Global Supply Chain Management,* by Matt Drake
- *Supply Chain Information Technology,* by David Olson
- *Improving Business Performance With Lean,* by James Bradley
- *Managing Commodity Price Risk,* by George A. Zsidisin

www.ingramcontent.com/pod-product-compliance
Lightning Source LLC
Chambersburg PA
CBHW071910200326
41519CB00016B/4553